TAKE A LOOK

An Introduction to the Experience of Art

Rosemary Davidson

Viking

Acknowledgments

I acknowledge with pleasure and gratitude a debt to many mentors and friends, dead and alive, who have in their different ways opened my eyes and mind to art:

Martha Steinitz, who on Saturday mornings in Leeds revealed a world of European visual and musical culture to the unknowing schoolgirl that I was. **Louis Porter**, who was the first person I knew who bought, hung, and talked about contemporary art. **Alan Davidson**, my brother, whose passion for Sienese paintings sent me to Italy with a guidebook specially written for me by him. **Janet Ward**, who bravely shared the discovery of Italian art from the back of a motor scooter. **Lynda Grier**, whose early patronage of Stanley Spencer taught me to follow my artistic hunch. **Kurt Rowland**, who showed me a way of looking that embraced the whole of our visual environment. **Jeannine and Reg Alton**, who, from when I was a student to the present day, have always leavened my ignorance and broadened my appreciation of art. And finally to all the artists who have contributed their works to my gallery and informally taught me much about the creative process.

On a practical level I should like to thank **Jo and Ken Brooks** for criticism and help, particularly with Chapter 11; **Katherine James** for patient checking and correcting; and **Barbara Brenchley** for comment and help with the glossary.

Library of Congress Cataloging-in-Publication Data
Davidson, Rosemary.
  Take a look: an introduction to the experience of art/by
Rosemary Davidson.
    p.   cm.
  Includes bibliographical references and index.
  Summary: Introduces the history, techniques, and functions of art
through discussion and reproductions of paintings, photographs,
drawings, and design elements. Includes activities and experiments.
  ISBN 0-670-84478-0
  1. Art—Juvenile literature. 2. Art—Technique—Juvenile
literature. [1. Art. 2. Art—Technique.] I. Title.
N7440.D37 1994   92–1180
701'.1—dc20   CIP
                                        AC

This is a Mirabel Book which was designed and produced by Cynthia Parzych Publishing, Inc.,
648 Broadway, New York, New York 10012

Designed by Malcolm Smythe/Camel Corps

Set in Palatino and Century Book Condensed

Printed and bound by Fournier A. Graficas S.A. in Spain

Contents

1 • Looking and Seeing

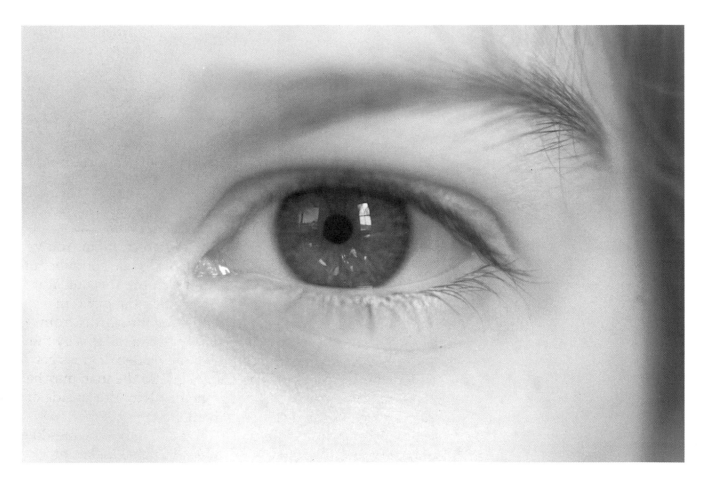

If You Think *Looking* Is the Same as *Seeing*— You're Wrong!

We've all got the same apparatus for looking: *eyes*. But what you see and what I see, looking at the same person or thing or place, may be very different. It all depends on what your brain does with the images that you take in through your eyes. And that depends on who you are:

- how old you are
- where you live
- how you've been brought up
- what you've already seen
- what you expect to see
- what you're interested in

It's as if we are all wearing different kinds of glasses that make us see things differently.

Experiment Time

What's this below? Right. It's part of a bicycle wheel. But you only know that it's part of a bicycle wheel because you already know what a whole bicycle looks like. If you'd never seen a bicycle in your life, you wouldn't know what this is.

What about this, above? What do you see? Do you see a little man dancing on the girl's finger? If you believe in gnomes and fairies, perhaps that's what you do see. But if you don't, you look again, this time harder, and perhaps you see the little man dancing along in the distance and the girl standing close to us, holding out her finger. You realize there's a big space between them. You've been able to use a number of clues to figure this out. You can see that the girl is in a field stretching away from you (you can tell this by the way the blades of grass get smaller). So the man may be dancing along the *far* side of the field.

You can only use clues like these if you've looked at pictures before.

What do these black dots make you think of?

Maybe they look like eyes to you. Or heads? Or glasses? Or flowers? Or wheels? Or an animal's ears? You can probably think of lots of other things they might be. The point is that your brain is always trying to make a connection between shapes you see and things you already know about.

Stare at This Ink Blot
for a While.
What Do You See?
A Man?
A Bird?
Something Else?

What you see depends on
you. But it's interesting to
know that when people look
at vague shapes they very
often see faces or people.
(You'll read more about this
farther on in the book.)

What has all this got to do with art? Quite a lot. Artists don't need to spell everything out, to show every detail. They can rely on us to do half the work! One of an artist's skills is knowing what *our* brains are going to do with the marks *they* have made. Artists have to be able to guess what we will see when we look at what they have done. But they can only do this up to a certain point. You and I are different, so we're bound to see the same picture differently—we even see colors differently.

What You See Depends on Who You Are

Here's a simple example. What is this below? Probably most people reading this book will say it's a goat. But when this drawing was shown to some children in Kenya, Africa, none of them said it was a goat. They had goats in their village and they knew perfectly well what those goats looked like. But all *their* goats had tails that turned *upward*—so this couldn't possibly be a goat.

Here's a more complicated example. When you look at this picture on the right you may see patterns like necklaces, or maybe you see mouths, or even hamburgers. . . . But an Australian Aborigine would know that this painting has to do with a rainmaking ritual that Aborigines have taken part in for thousands of years. An Aborigine would see water cascading from one water hole to the next, and the tracks of a boy and a possum out looking for food. He or she would look at the picture as if looking down at the ground from the air.

This picture, called Children's Water Dreaming with Possum Story, *was painted in acrylic paint on a piece of hardboard by an Australian Aborigine named Old Mick Tjakamara. Acrylic paint and hardboard are modern, but the ideas in the picture are ancient.*

8

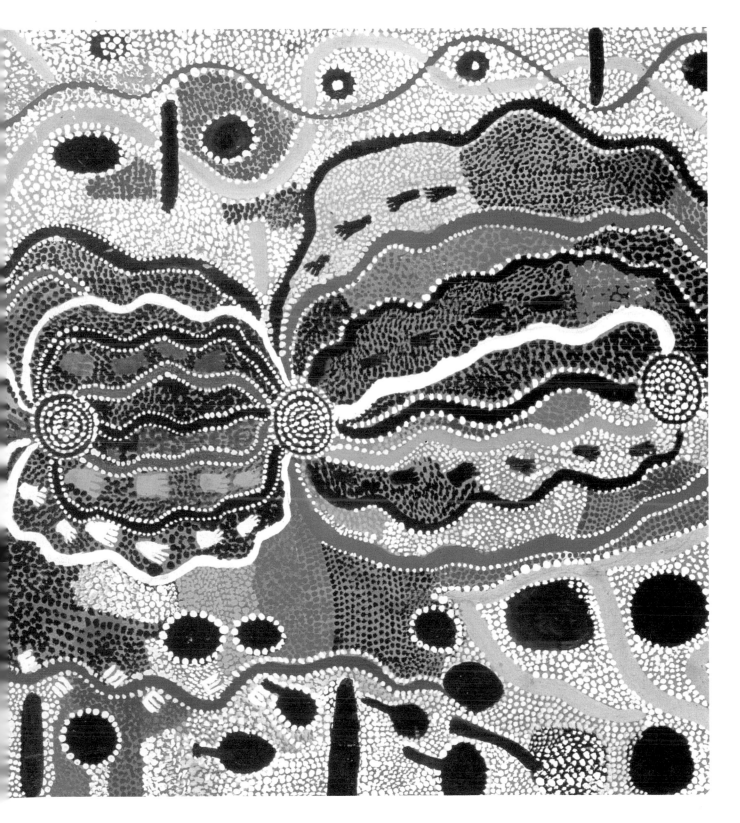

What You See Depends on What You *Expect* to See

Huh?

Take a look at this drawing.

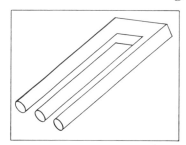

Even if you didn't know it was a tuning fork, you'd see pretty quickly that there was something wrong with it. It's an impossible object. Try to figure out why. Your brain keeps wanting to turn it into a regular tuning fork, because that's what you expect to see.

Take a quick look at this sign and read it out loud.

PARIS
IN THE
THE SPRING

Now take a more careful look and read it aloud again. The first time you probably read what you were expecting to find. The second time you read what was really there.

You See What Interests You

How we look at something depends on what we're interested in. There's a special kind of camera that can photograph the way your eyes move when you're looking at a picture. It makes a map of your eye movements. The map shows how your eyes have moved around the picture and which parts of it you've been looking at most because they interested you most.

Above is a painting called Stowing Sail, Bahamas *by the American artist Winslow Homer. From the map of the eye movements below you can see how the eyes of the person looking at the painting kept moving between the two boats. But most lines are over the man on the right, which means the person's eyes kept coming back to that man.*

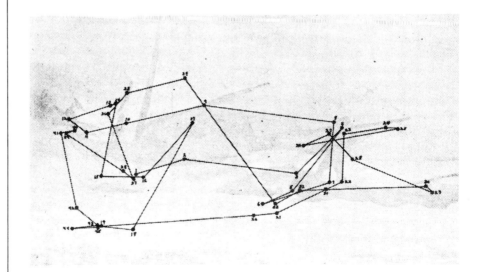

Magritte's Magic

René Magritte lived nearly all his life (1898–1967) in Belgium. He liked to paint the ordinary objects of his everyday life—loaves of bread, boots, his pipe, and his bowler hat—in such an odd way that they give you a shock and make you look again. Did you do a double-take when you looked at *Le Modèle Rouge,* left?

"When I was a child," Magritte said, "a little girl and I used to play in the old cemetery . . . where an artist from the city would be painting in a picturesque walk with broken stone columns scattered among the dead leaves. It seemed to me that the art of painting was vaguely magical."

His paintings give you the same feeling of a mad, magical world as Lewis Carroll does in *Alice's Adventures in Wonderland.*

Magritte's pipe and bowler hat became so famous through his paintings that not long ago they were sold for a lot of money at an art auction.

You See What the Artist *Wants* You to See

What we see and how we look at a picture depend not only on who we are, what we expect to see, and what we're interested in. There's something else that's very important. And that's the way the artist builds up the picture, composes it with shapes and colors. A skilled artist can make us look at a particular part first, and can urge our eyes in a certain direction.

But Mr Magnolia —

poor Mr Magnolia!

— Mr Magnolia

has

only one boot . . .

Hey —

This is a picture by Quentin Blake from his story **Mr. Magnolia.** *The natural tendency of our eyes is to start looking at a picture somewhere over on the left. But this time we start looking over on the right, where Mr. Magnolia is standing by the window, because there's so much going on in that part of the picture. This is just what Blake wants to happen, because he doesn't want us to notice until* after *we've looked at Mr. Magnolia that the little girl is coming into the room.*

2 • *What's Art For?*

If somebody asked you "What's food for?" or "What are houses for?" you'd find it easy to answer. But the question "What's art for?" isn't so easy to answer.

When you set out to make a drawing or a painting for yourself, you're not usually thinking about "making art," but about doing something *for a reason*. You may want to record something that has happened—like a volcano blowing up. Or you may want to illustrate a story you've read, or written yourself. You may want to try making a picture of your friend. You may want to do something different, like designing a poster or making a necklace. Or you may just want to settle down with paper, crayons or felt-tip pens, and a pair of scissors, and have fun with them. Whatever you do, there'll be a *secret ingredient*. That's the piece of yourself you put into whatever you're doing. We all do things in our own

way, choosing this color and not that, this shape and not another. You could call it a kind of language that's all our own.

These are just the sorts of things that artists do. In the past they were often employed by a rich person, by a ruler, or by the Church. They might have been painting a wall in a church or palace, illustrating a legend or setting down the scene of a battle. They could have been painting a series of pictures to go over an altar. They could have been making figures to be buried with an Egyptian pharaoh, to go with him into the next world. Like you, they could have been doing things just for fun. They, too, were using their own "language." After a while, we come to recognize the work of an artist by his or her "language." We call that "style."

In the next few pages you can see examples of some of the important ways in which people have made art.

Art Is For . . . Telling a Story

The stories that artists tell are about all sorts of things—they come from the different religions of the world, from the legends of the ancient Greeks, from India, China, and the North American Indians. Artists also tell stories from the 20th century.

One of the best-known modern storyteller-artists is N. C. Wyeth (1882–1945). His son Andrew, also an artist, tape-recorded some of his memories of his father. Andrew Wyeth said this about the *McKeon's Graft* (*Train Robbery*) painting on this page:

"He painted it in one morning. At that time he was doing pictures of adventure stories and he could make up any subject he wanted as long as it had to do with the West and was something with a lot of drama. He got the idea of this train robbery, went up to the studio, and just painted it like mad. It was finished by noon."

N. C. Wyeth was very skilled at knowing what to concentrate on and what to leave out. He painted only a small part of the train, just enough for us to recognize it as a train. He concentrated everything on the figure of the robber, whose flying collar and foot stepping forward make us feel he's still moving. All you see of the passengers is a glimpse. Everything else is left vague—the second robber clambering up holding a knife in his mouth, the landscape, the steam-filled foreground.

Wyeth liked illustrating what he called "a good yarn": *Treasure Island*, *Robin Hood*, and *The Last of the Mohicans*. He also liked to do paintings of dramatic stories he himself imagined, especially about the Wild West.

Art Is For . . . Making Pictures of People

People are interested in people. So portraits are a form of art that people take to with enthusiasm—both painting them and looking at them. Also, portraits have been, and still are, a good way for artists to earn their living.

This portrait is of Ranuccio Farnese and we know that it was painted in 1542. He was then 12 years old, studying at the Italian University of Padua. He was already prior of an important institution in Venice, and at 15 he was made a cardinal of the Catholic Church, an even more important position. Knowing about his life, you start to notice things about the picture. His clothes are very grand for a boy. But his face looks very young, he seems rather shy, and his ears stick out.

The artist who painted the portrait was Titian (about 1485–1576). He painted people of all ages. He was particularly good at painting children and teenagers. We know that he painted Ranuccio partly from life and partly from memory. Surely he must have painted the face while the boy was there in front of him.

Photographs of People

Photographic portraits are now much more common than painted portraits. A photographer can show a person's character by choosing a particular angle, by arranging the light in a certain way, and by catching a particular facial expression. This photograph is of one of the best-known faces in the world. It is Mother Teresa of Calcutta.

Art Is For . . . Recording a Scene

The scenes that artists have recorded range from battles to picnics, from murders to miracles. When a scene appeals to an artist's imagination—because it is interesting to that artist in a particular way, because it helps him or her to do the things he or she wants to do—then we are likely to get a good picture.

Georges Seurat (1859–1891) found the scene he wanted by the River Seine near Paris, France. There was an island, "la

Grande Jatte," where people went to enjoy themselves on Sunday. The light was special, reflected from the river. There were people walking, sitting, lying down, fishing, playing the trumpet. There were trees, children, boats, parasols, dogs, even a monkey now

and then. So there were lots of different shapes and colors to play around with. Seurat made many small drawings and paintings of the people and animals he saw. Then he experimented with different ways of putting them together. A picture like this is a combination of things seen, remembered, and imagined.

If you look closely, you'll see that for most of the picture he put the paint on in little dots of different colors. Seurat was very interested in colors and how they worked together. He thought colors worked better if you put them next to each other in dots than if you mixed them together. This is one of the first paintings to be done in that way, using "pointillisme" (*pointe* is French for "point" or "dot").

This is the kind of picture that leads your eye around from one mini-scene to another, from one character to another. It invites you to make up stories about the people. In fact, someone did. James Lapine and Stephen Sondheim wrote a musical based on this picture called *Sunday in the Park with George*. The painting comes to life on the stage—the characters "form" the painting. At the end of each act all the characters sing:

> "Sunday
> By the blue
> Purple yellow red water
> On the green
> Orange violet mass
> Of the grass
> In our perfect park."

This painting, A Sunday Afternoon on the Island of "la Grande Jatte," *is quite large —
6 feet 9 inches high and 10 feet wide. It was painted in 1886, when Seurat was 27 years old. (He died when he was only 31.)*

Art Is For . . . Fun

When you were very young, you probably spent time messing around with paper and paints, sand, and Play-Doh. You were experimenting, finding out what happened when you handled these materials—and enjoying yourself. You may think that artists always know what they're doing, that they've already learned how to do things. But in fact the greatest artists keep on experimenting and learning. Often the way they do this is by playing around with materials.

Some artists let us see the way they do this. One of these was Paul Klee (1879–1940). He came from Switzerland and was one of the most playful and humorous artists of this century. His son, Felix, tells us that he produced about 10,000 paintings and drawings in the course of his life!

Klee called this picture on the right *Tomcat's Turf* (meaning his territory). His tomcat roamed over a landscape that included a moored boat, a watermill, a red sun, green fields, and—a mouse. Klee liked to cut up his pictures and rearrange the parts. In *Tomcat's Turf* he switched the upper and lower parts around, so that now the mouse, high up in the green fields, appears to be lording it over the cat, down below in the blue sky. Perhaps the big letter F is for Fritzi,

the name of his cat. What could the B be for? Bern, the town where Klee lived? A town mouse from Bern on holiday in the country?

Klee at Home

Klee was able to produce so much because he had a devoted wife in the background who protected him from all interruptions, right? Wrong! When Felix was small, it was his father who stayed at home, looked after him, and did the cooking. Klee painted

his pictures in the kitchen, stirring the soup with the end of his paintbrush. He loved animals, particularly cats. He kept them, wrote about them, put them in his pictures, and once even signed a letter with his tomcat Fritzi's paw! This is a photograph of Fritzi in 1921.

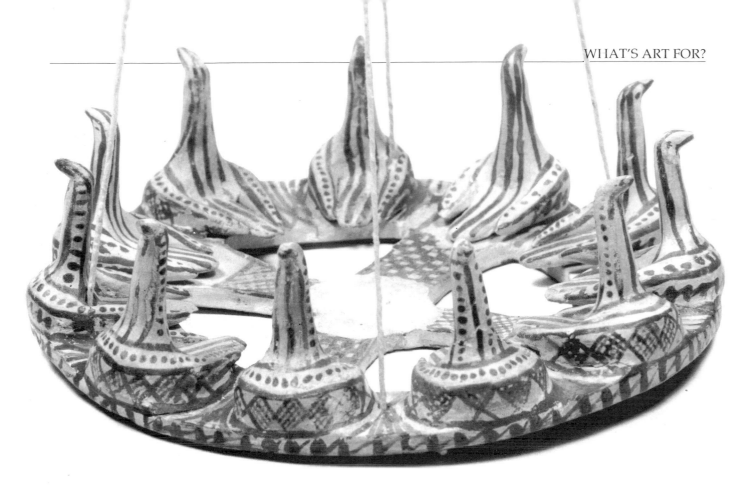

Art Is For . . . Magic

People have made images for use in magic as far back as history goes—back at least to the paintings our ancestors made in caves 15,000 years ago. The objects used for magic are sometimes rather mysterious to us—we don't really know how they were used.

This wheel is one of those mysterious objects. It was found in Greece and is about 2,700 years old. Nobody has ever found another one, but there are pictures of wheels like it on Greek vases. It's made of terracotta and the striped birds are wrynecks (a kind of woodpecker). The wheel is only 11 inches across. The holes for strings show that it was meant to be hung, like a mobile, or to be swung around. Some people think it's connected with the idea that a young woman could find her lost lover by spinning a wheel. Whatever it was used for, we do know that circles are often sacred.

Magic Circles

Scattered around the world, in Britain, Ireland, Scandinavia, North America, and Asia, there are mysterious stone circles of great age. In Britain the best known is Stonehenge, in the south of England. It is 100 feet across. It too is a mystery,

but people think it was built about 4,000 years ago for religious ceremonies that had to do with the sun or for studying the movements of the moon.

The Native Americans of the Southwest also made sacred circles, called "medicine wheels," used in their "medicine" (magic).

Art Is For . . . Decoration

Most of us want to make our mark on our surroundings. We may decorate our bodies. We may arrange things in a pattern. We may weave cloth in a variety of patterns—for clothes, wall hangings, or rugs. We may make everyday things, such as pots, glasses, and knives, in beautiful shapes and decorate them.

What you do with your surroundings and your personal possessions depends on who you are, where you are, and what kind of life you lead. You may decorate your room with posters, or your pencil case with stickers. This isn't art. But it *is* something to do with our wish to make things around us more interesting or more beautiful than they need be for practical purposes, and to make them "special" to us.

If you were a Japanese person in the 18th century, one of your special personal possessions might have been a *netsuke* (pronounced NET-soo-kay). At that time the Japanese wore kimonos, without pockets. So how did they carry their money, their tobacco pipes, and their writing implements? They put them in little pouches or cases and hung them by cords from their sash or belt. And they fastened the cords with a *netsuke*, which is a small toggle usually carved out of wood or ivory. This drawing by Tori Kiyonaga

(1752–1815) shows a man wearing a *netsuke* in the form of an octopus, for holding his tobacco pouch.

Netsuke Toggles

Netsuke were miniature sculptures, very often in the form of an animal. They had to be very smooth, with no sharp ears or claws or tail that might catch on the kimono. And, of course, they became even smoother with use. Some of the *netsuke* carvers were

famous and signed their work, just as painters and sculptors do. There are still artists carving *netsuke* in

Japan today, and there's even one artist in the north of England making them.

This *netsuke*, in the form of a rat, is the same size as in the photograph. It was beautifully carved out of ivory by the well-known Japanese artist Masanao of Kyoto, in Japan, who was making netsuke between 1781 and 1800.

3 • *Magic and Making Things Happen*

We don't really know how or when people began to make images. But we do know that the oldest images we've found have to do with people's religions and beliefs.

Cave Paintings of Animals

About 15,000 to 17,000 years ago, in what is now Spain and France, people drew and painted animals on the walls of underground caves. Many of these animals were the ones they hunted for food—bison, bulls, cows, and deer. Some people think these paintings of animals illustrated the legends of the tribes that made the pictures. Other people think they made the pictures to help in their hunting, so they'd be more likely to catch their prey—a kind of hunting magic. Either way, the caves where the paintings were found were not the places where these people lived (we know this because no remains of food were found there). They were sacred places.

This galloping horse is in the caves at Lascaux, in southwest France.

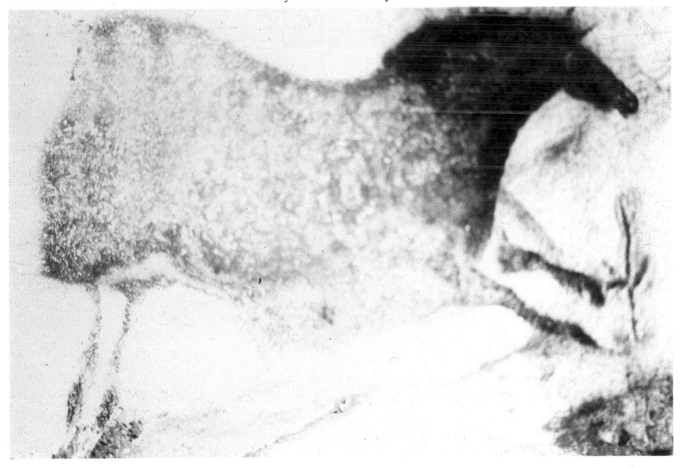

People in many different parts of the world have believed in this kind of hunting magic—for example, the Bushmen of southern Africa and the Aborigines of Australia. Rock paintings of animals have been found in caves in France, Spain, North America, Africa, and Australia.

This bull with long horns is in the Great Hall of the Bulls at Lascaux. It's surrounded by painted arrows. They could be part of the hunting magic.

Is What You See the Same as What You Know?

The people who made these cave pictures showed the animals from the side. But sometimes they added something you couldn't actually see. If you look at a deer sideways, you see only one group of antlers (because those on the other side of the head are hidden behind the first group). But these cave painters knew that the deer really had a second group of antlers, so they showed them as well, as below. Children often do that in their drawings, and so have artists in the 20th century.

Children Who Made Great Cave Discoveries

It's not just grown-ups who make important discoveries. It was a small girl who first saw the bulls painted on the roof of the cave at Altamira in Spain that her father was exploring. Her father hadn't thought of looking up! That was in 1879.

In 1940, four boys were walking their dog at Lascaux, in southwest France. When their dog disappeared into a crack in the rocks, they climbed down to rescue him and found themselves in a big underground gallery. By the light of matches they could see that the cave walls were covered with extraordinary paintings of animals. They found their dog and went home.

After a second visit, with a lamp, they told their teacher. Then everyone wanted to come and see—the people who lived nearby, journalists, and photographers. The boys camped just outside to protect "their" cave.

Although Lascaux has some of the most famous cave paintings yet discovered, you can no longer visit them because people's breath damages the delicate artwork.

Using Magic

We may think that it's only other people in other countries at other times who have used objects in a magical way. But think for a moment! You probably know someone who wears a lucky charm around his or her neck. Charms are pretty things, but they're also meant to bring good luck. You may have seen a St. Christopher medal in a car, like the one below on the left. St. Christopher is the Christian patron saint of travelers (although he's not an "official" saint anymore), and is supposed to protect them on journeys. Skiers used to carry an Ullr medal (below right) to protect them from breaking their neck or leg. Ullr (also known as Ull, or Uller) was an ancient Nordic nature god who is always shown on skis and with a bow and arrow. He has been mixed up in people's minds with St. Ulrich, a 10th-century bishop of Augsburg, who is said to give protection against natural catastrophes and dangerous journeys.

The ancient Egyptians thought a scarab (a kind of beetle) was particularly lucky and made copies of them in large numbers out of glass or stone for people to keep. People still use scarabs as lucky charms today. Some people even carry a special pebble in their pocket, which they can secretly touch and turn over to bring them luck. Perhaps even today we believe in magic more than we think we do.

Sorcerers, magicians, medicine men, or shamans: in primitive societies it was believed that these people performed magic—for good or evil. They didn't work directly on the person concerned, but on an image of that person (a doll, for example), or on something to do with the person— hair, or a piece of clothing. They may have tried to cure a person of an illness, or tried to do harm. Many of the objects connected with these activities—masks, carved figures, sticks, and boards—are made with great skill, and beautifully decorated.

(Right) This is a rattle, not for a baby but for a shaman (a kind of medicine man). It was made by a Native American out of wood and carved with a bear's head. It is for frightening bad spirits away. It comes from the northwest coast of America.

The Evil Eye

People believed that witches and sorcerers could "put the evil eye" on someone. You could protect yourself by wearing a little metal hand (in North Africa), or clothes with little mirrors sewn into them (in India).

The ancient Egyptian *udjatti* symbol means "two eyes." One eye represented the sun and the other the moon.

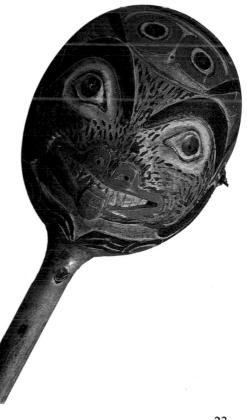

A Dead Man's Luggage

Many people believe that when you die you go on to another life. The ancient Egyptians, for example, believed that when people died their spirit, their "*ka*," left the body, but would return. They thought they'd go on needing the same kinds of things they needed in this life. So they supplied their dead with "survival kits" for the next life— pots, tools, games, musical instruments, food, and drink.

With kings, queens, and nobles they also buried fine furniture and clothes, jewelry, and even models of workmen and servants to look after them. They prepared the body of the dead person so that it would not decay and would be ready for the spirit to return to it. They embalmed it with spices and wrapped it up in bandages to make a mummy. (The ancient Egyptians also made mummies of cats, birds, and fish because they were sacred animals.) Since they wanted to honor a dead king or queen, the objects they made to put in the tomb were very rich and beautiful. By doing all this, the ancient Egyptians thought they could make sure that all would be well with the dead person in the future life.

In ancient China 3,000 years ago, they did the same kind of thing. A person's wealth

was measured by the number of horses and chariots he had. In 1969, archeologists dug up a tomb containing hundreds of bronze horses and chariots—so they knew it must be the tomb of an important person. They soon discovered who he was: the name of Governor Chang was written on several of the figures. Above is one of the bronze horses from Governor Chang's tomb. It has been called "the flying horse" because it is so much up in the air and looks as if it's moving swiftly. The way a horse's legs move when it's galloping is quite complicated, and many artists have gotten it wrong. This artist got it nearly right! The hoof that's touching the ground is resting on a swallow. No wonder the horse is neighing with surprise!

This wooden head is of Anubis, the Egyptian god of embalming. He has a man's body and a jackal's head. His task: to watch over the dead person and the tomb. The mask is about 2,300 years old.

What Do *You* Think?

Tombs can tell us a lot about people who lived long ago and what they believed in. But some people believe that by digging up tombs we are disturbing the dead.

What do *you* think about that? Is it all worth it because of what we learn? Or should we respect the dead?

Images of Gods and Spirits

People of many different religions or beliefs have made images of their god or gods, or of the spirits that were (and are) important to them. Often these were the spirits of their ancestors—their grandparents, great-grandparents, great-great-grandparents, and so on. Sometimes these images helped people to worship and think about their gods. But sometimes people worshiped the image itself. They prayed to the image to make things happen. They might pray to a statue of their god of war to make them win a battle, or to a fertility god to help them have a child. In some religions (the Jewish and Muslim religions, for instance) it is forbidden to make images of God.

(Below) The work of the modern Zimbabwean sculptor Joseph Ndandarika (1940–91) links up with the ancient traditions of African art— in it we see humans as part of the wider world of nature, and linked to their ancestral spirits.

The terracotta head above may have been used for ancestor worship, or may have been put in a man's tomb about 2,300 years ago in the Nok Valley, Nigeria. It was discovered by a tin miner in 1954. Other male heads like this have been found by miners in the same region, and once by some schoolboys making a hockey field. The heads are usually the same size as real heads or a little smaller. They have beautifully modeled eyes, noses, and mouths, and often very complicated hairstyles.

Totems

Totems are a way of showing the spirits of people's ancestors. We think of people and animals as different—while accepting that both are part of nature. In the past, people thought of themselves and animals and plants and rocks as much more closely linked to each other. Spirits could take the form of any object, animal, or person. A group of people all related to one another might believe that they were all descended from a particular animal. Sometimes they believed that a particular animal had helped their human ancestor, perhaps even saved his or her life. That animal, perhaps a bear, a raven, or a killer whale, became their sign and was sacred. It was called a totem. As a member of your group, you might make a carving of your totem and put it in front of your house, or you might draw it in the sand, or make an image of it as a mask for your face. You might even mime it or dance it. It was a sacred secret that you shared with the other members of your group.

The man who found this in Alaska about a hundred years ago was a bishop. He may not have known at first what it was. It is a wooden mask, 19 inches high, in the form of a seal basking on its back in the water, seen from above. The face is the human soul, returning to its animal home.

This totem of a thunderbird is from Canada. It's beautifully carved and painted. Can you see how its front looks like a face?

This enormous raven totem used to stand in front of the house of a chief of the Haida people on the northwest coast of North America. When the chief's son was in his eighties, he pointed to the place where the totem had been and said, "It is customary for the nephews of a chief to keep him supplied with halibut. But do you think this is done anymore for me? Not one piece! They want to go to the movies!"

Although the totem no longer belongs to the chief, it's still used for storytelling in the museum where it now stands.

This painted wooden shaman's mask (with real human hair) comes from the northwest coast of North America. The shamans designed the masks and sometimes carved them too. This is a very fierce one. Many of the masks are cleverly designed, with parts that move and fold back when you pull strings.

Masks

Masks were also a way of representing spirits. They were often used for religious ceremonies and they were usually strange and frightening. The person wearing the mask "became" the spirit or god in the ceremony. You can find masks of this kind in many different parts of the world—the demon masks of the Tibetans and the animal masks of the Native Americans, for example.

In Africa, chiefs used to wear animal masks as a sign of power. Some masks were made to be slung on their belts and hung from the left hip (sort of like a gun holster) or worn around the neck. Magicians in Africa and Borneo sometimes wear masks when they're trying to cure people's illnesses.

People also wore masks in the theater, and sometimes still do. In the time of the ancient Greeks, about 3,000 years ago, actors always wore masks. They were either "tragic" masks or "comic" masks—so the audience was quite clear what kind of play it was about to see. Actors in the traditional Japanese "Noh" plays of 600 years ago always wore masks, and still do. Today people sometimes wear masks at carnivals and Halloween parties, so that they can behave as they like, without anyone knowing who they are.

Face Painting

Another way of making yourself look frightening is to paint your face. Dancers often paint their faces. The Aborigines of Australia do it, and so do the dancers of Papua New Guinea, and the Kathakali dancers of India.

Maybe you've tried it too. When your face is painted to look like a lion or a wolf, you might find yourself acting like a lion or a wolf. So you can understand the effect masks or painted faces have on dancers or people taking part in a ceremony, and on the people watching them.

This young dancer from Papua New Guinea has had his face painted. He's wearing a fur cap with bead decoration, and cowrie shells around his neck. One of the older dancers painted his face for him.

4 • Telling a Story

When we think of stories, we usually think of books—and of *reading* stories. But it's only in the last hundred years or so that most people in the developed world have been able to read. That doesn't mean that people did without stories. They told them to each other.

Another good way of telling stories is through pictures. The ancient Greeks told stories in the pictures on their pots. The Romans often carved a series of pictures in stone—rather like a comic strip. You can tell a story by embroidering pictures in a long strip, which is what the people who made the Bayeux Tapestry did when they told the story of the invasion of England by the Normans in 1066.

The Minotaur was a monster that was half man and half bull. This was a popular story 2,500 years ago on the island of Crete in the Mediterranean. From that time on, Greek potters often illustrated it on their pots. Here, the hero Theseus is shown slaying the Minotaur.

The Romans liked to make stone carvings of real-life events—like the earthquake that took place in Pompeii in 62 A.D.

The city buildings and statues are moving . . . with the earthquake.

Stories Galore

The stories that you can "read" on pots and in paintings, carvings, and tapestries may be very ancient, or quite modern. The old stories come from the myths and legends of ancient peoples—stories that have been handed on sometimes by word of mouth, sometimes written down. These kinds of stories are about heroes and warriors, monsters and dragons, kings and queens, journeys and battles. You've probably come across some of them already—the voyages of the Greek Ulysses, and perhaps the story of the monster Minotaur. Stories are important because they tell people about their past, and give them a sense of their own history. Stories give people a sense of who they are.

(Above) *The Japanese told stories by painting them on silk scrolls and folding screens. These too were often about wars and battles. Japan was ruled 400 years ago by warriors. They commissioned artists to paint stories of their victories in rich colors on screens, to decorate their castles. Here is part of one of those screens, showing a palace scene. The artist cut the wall away so that you can see what's going on inside the palace.*

The gateway and tower collapse . . . and a mule cart escapes just in time.

EXER ACI TV:

The Bayeux Tapestry

1

The Bayeux Tapestry tells the story of the bitter war between King Harold of England and Duke William of Normandy, which ended with the Battle of Hastings in 1066. Harold lost the battle and the Normans conquered England.

The Bayeux Tapestry is about 230 feet long and 20 inches wide. It's not really a tapestry at all (a real tapestry is woven) but is made of strips of embroidered linen joined together, each about 8 feet long. We don't know for sure who made it. But people think it may have been made in England between 1070 and 1080, A.D. by teams of embroiderers at the famous School of

Embroidery in Canterbury, and then shipped over to Bayeux in Normandy.

There are no speech balloons, just a few words in Latin describing what's going on. But the figures are shown so vividly that you can easily understand what's going on without any words.

In this exciting episode, Duke William's Norman soldiers, in their suits of chain mail (**1**), are galloping to attack King Harold's English foot soldiers from both sides. The English are making a "shield wall" (**2**) and fighting with spears, arrows, and axes. This was a fierce and terrible battle that went on all day.

Tintin in America

Hergé, the Belgian artist-storyteller, wrote all his Tintin stories as comic strips. (There are 24 stories and they've been translated into 45 languages!) If you compare this part of *Tintin in America* with the part of the Bayeux Tapestry on these pages, you may make some interesting discoveries. Look at the way Hergé outlined his horses and people. Then look at the way the makers of the Bayeux Tapestry did it. You'll find they both used color in the same way—areas of clear color against a plain background.

Look! There he goes!...Escaping on a horse... someone must have tipped him off when I arrived in town...

OK, Bobby Smiles, we're right behind you!

You can't escape, my friend! I'll truss you like a turkey!

BANG BANG

"Reading" Pictures

Many of the stories in art come from the religions of the world. Pictures are a good way of telling religious stories both for those who can't read and for those who can. They make a story stay in your mind. The Christian religion, for example, has hundreds of stories of saints, from St. Francis, who preached to the birds and tamed a wolf, to St. George, a warrior saint and martyr who, according to legend, fought and slew a dragon and became the patron saint of England.

Artists all over Europe have painted religious pictures since the Middle Ages, but the painters working in Italy in the 14th and 15th centuries painted some of the most interesting and beautiful ones ever. Sometimes they painted the story of a saint on several small wooden panels, sometimes as a mural on one or more walls. And sometimes they painted different parts of the story all in the same picture.

This painting tells the story of a Christian hermit, St. Anthony (with a halo), who decided to visit St. Paul, another hermit.

The story starts in the top left corner, with the old hermit setting out on his travels. On the way he meets a centaur (half man, half horse), a creature from an older religion. The centaur is holding a palm branch and is beating his breast—meaning perhaps that he wants to leave his pagan ways behind and become a Christian. *St. Anthony blesses him. Then he travels on, down the side of a dark wood, and finally meets up with St. Paul. The two old men embrace.*

Stefano di Giovanni, known as Sassetta, painted this picture in the 15th century (about 550 years ago) in Italy, near Siena. The picture is on a small wooden panel. The story is easy to follow, and the way Sassetta arranged the different elements, and the colors he used, make it very beautiful to look at.

"Reading" Windows and Doors

In France and England, in the Middle Ages, Christians built churches and cathedrals with enormous windows. They filled these windows with colored glass—stained glass, as it's called. These windows often told the great stories of the Christian religion. They showed the stories of Adam and Eve, of Noah and the Flood, of the lives of Jesus and the saints. You can read these window-picture stories like a book, if you know how to. You usually start at the bottom on the left, read across to the right, and then start on the next line of pictures above that.

Bronze doors made for churches were also used in Italy and Spain for telling Bible stories. Some doors had as many as 48 panels, each with a different episode. You are usually meant to read these from the top down, like the lines of a book, but there are some that you read upward, like stained-glass windows.

Here is the story of the angel coming to tell the shepherds about the birth of Jesus, a story that every Christian in the Middle Ages would know well: the Annunciation to the Shepherds. The important parts are white and yellow. The shepherds are dressed in the same kind of clothing that people in the Middle Ages looking at this stained-glass window might have been wearing. One of the shepherds is playing the bagpipes, and the dog is guarding the sheep.

For the Record

Some stories in art are about things that really happened—wars and battles, earthquakes and floods, disasters and accidents. Photography was not invented until about 150 years ago, so before that it was painters who recorded events. In the past, artists were paid to produce portraits and religious paintings for the king, the Church, or rich people—these were their patrons. Rulers hired artists to record their victories and to make them look splendid.

But in the last 200 years, artists have begun

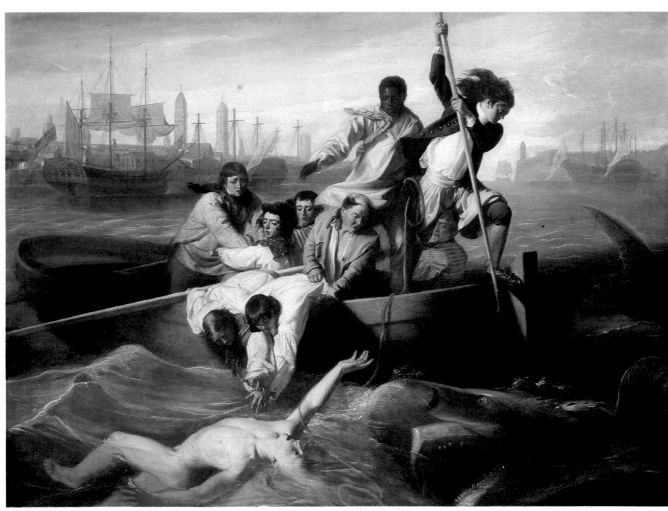

Will the boy be saved? Will the shark get him? This painting, Watson and the Shark, *tells a true horror story. In 1749 a young British sailor named Brook Watson was swimming in Havana harbor in the Caribbean. He was attacked by a shark, which first tore off all the flesh from one leg and then bit off his foot. The picture shows the moment when the shark was attacking for the third time.*

Young Brook Watson did escape the shark's jaws. He became a successful merchant, a member of the British Parliament, and Lord Mayor of London—with a wooden leg. He had this picture painted to hang in his old school, "that it might serve a most useful Lesson to Youth." (What do you think that lesson was?)

John Singleton Copley, who painted this picture, had never been to Havana, but he studied maps and drawings to get the background right. When this very large and dramatic painting was shown at the Royal Academy in London, the public loved it. Copley must have liked it too, for he painted a copy to keep for himself.

to earn their money in other ways as well—from exhibitions and private sales. And so they have been less dependent on getting work from wealthy patrons. They have been free to show in their paintings what they really felt about the events they recorded. The Spanish artist Francisco Goya (1746–1828) showed the horror of war and the misery of poor people in his pictures, as well as painting official royal portraits.

These painters were not just recording an event—they were also giving the feel of the event, and making the picture interesting *as a picture*.

At the beginning of the 19th century, there was a war between France and Spain. During this war the French took Spanish hostages—and shot some of them on May 3, 1808. The Spanish artist Goya painted a picture of this six years after it had happened, but when you look at it you feel he must have done it on the spot—like a war photographer. He called it simply The Third of May, 1808.

The Story of Guernica

Pablo Picasso (1881–1973) painted this enormous picture (it's 12 feet high and 25 feet wide) at the time of the Spanish Civil War in the 1930s. There was an air raid on the small Basque town of Guernica. No one was expecting it, and many people were killed. Once you've seen Picasso's painting, you do not forget the story of Guernica.

The picture now hangs in the new museum of 20th-century art in Madrid, but it hasn't always hung in Spain. Picasso refused to live in Spain after the Civil War, and would not allow his painting to be shown there while the dictator General Franco was in power. For years *Guernica* hung in New York. In 1981, after Franco died and Spain had become a democracy, the painting was taken to Madrid. It was too late for Picasso to see this happen, since he had died in 1973.

Picasso put all his feelings about the horror of war into this figure of a woman with her arms raised. (Perhaps he was thinking too of an earthquake he was in as a child.) Look at the hostage about to be shot in Goya's painting on page 37. He seems to have been painted with the same feeling.

Cops and Robbers

People have always found tales of cops and robbers exciting. The Australian artist Sidney Nolan painted a series of 27 pictures based on the life of Ned Kelly, a young bushranger (bandit) who was hanged in 1880. Every Australian knows about Ned Kelly. He and his gang were a legend in their own time.

The Ned Kelly Story

Ned Kelly was the son of an Irish ex-convict who had a small farm not far from Melbourne. By the time Ned was 12 he had left school, his father had died, and he was the head of the family. The police caught him helping someone steal a horse, and put him in jail for 3 years.

He was a tough man, an excellent horseman, and a deadly shot. When he got out of jail, he and his brother and their friends formed a gang and became outlaws. They robbed banks and fought the police, but were friendly toward ordinary people, and were always courteous to women. Finally there was a shoot-out and Ned was taken prisoner. He was condemned to death and hanged. He was just 26 and he became a folk hero.

Ned had a black, box-like metal helmet made for himself. (It was quilted inside and quite comfortable.) He wore it when he was out on horseback with his gun. In Ned Kelly, *Nolan found he could contrast this black shape very well with the wide yellow landscape and the blue sky.*

In The Chase, *Nolan painted the policeman galloping off in the opposite direction. Ned's red-and-yellow-striped helmet and body covering, and his long gun, make him look like a medieval knight charging in a tournament. The paint Nolan used was not artist's oil paint but an ordinary enamel house paint.*

Ned Kelly in the courthouse, with the judge, the jury, and 8 policemen in The Trial.

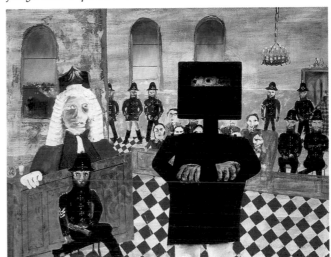

The Painter in Rubber Boots

Sidney Nolan (1917–1992) was born in Melbourne, Australia. His father's family originally came from Ireland (like Ned Kelly's family). When Nolan grew up, he took all sorts of jobs to earn money while he painted. Once, when he was working on an asparagus farm, he turned up at an art exhibition in Melbourne wearing his work clothes and an old pair of rubber boots—quite an odd thing to do in those days.

As a child he had seen Kelly's "armor" on display in Melbourne, and his own grandfather used to tell him tales of when he was a sergeant chasing the Kelly Gang. Nolan was fascinated by the story. In 1946 he went to see Jim Kelly, one of Ned's brothers, by then an old man, who had been in the gang.

"Hello," Nolan said. "Are you Ned Kelly's brother, Mr. Kelly?"

"Yes, I am. But it's none of your business!"

Nolan said once, "Really the Kelly paintings are secretly about myself."

He was living with friends called John and Sunday Reed. When he left, he gave all the Kelly paintings to Sunday—just like that. Some years later, Sunday gave them to the National Gallery of Art in Canberra, Australia.

Nolan painted many pictures with Australian themes—landscapes and pictures of people—but his most exciting are the Ned Kelly series.

Beginnings and Endings

In magazines, and sometimes in this book, there may be a special box, or something large printed in the center of two pages, and you find that's the part you look at first.

Sometimes it works that way with paintings, too. In a picture there may be a "route" that your eye follows because the artist has planned the composition of the picture to make this happen. In the picture on page 34, the route starts in the top left-hand corner and winds on down to the bottom.

With some pictures you find yourself wandering around, piecing a story together from one part here and another part there. This happens with Picasso's *Guernica*.

Pieter Bruegel the Elder was also a great one for cramming his pictures with all sorts of mini-scenes. In *Children's Games* (below) you can start looking wherever you like and it's bound to be interesting. There are 80 different games shown in the picture, although here you see only part of it.

This picture, about 4 feet by 6 feet, was painted in oils by Pieter Bruegel the Elder (1525–1569) in the Netherlands. See how many games you can recognize in the picture.

5 • Face to Face

Faces fascinate us. A newborn baby is already able to recognize the pattern of a face—the eyes, nose, and mouth. We see faces in all sorts of things—in trees, in houses, in clouds, for example. Maybe you see a face in the moon—that's where the idea of "the man in the moon" came from. It's as if we're naturally "programmed" to see faces.

(Left) *This little girl, drawn by Asun Balzola, sees a face in the moon. Not the man in the moon, but the woman in the moon!*

(Right) *The artist Nan Youngman saw a face in a house and called her painting of it* The Laughing Shed.

The cartoonist Mel Calman saw a face in a light switch, and added a body to it. Cover up the body. Do you still see the face?

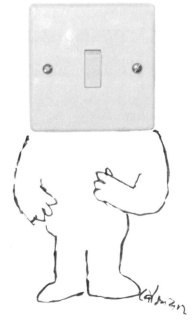

People living a thousand years ago in Sweden used these handy pieces of wood, ivory, and bone to carve heads. Each one is different, perhaps because the materials the carvers started out with were different. Try making a head out of the cardboard tube from a roll of toilet paper or from a plastic bottle or an egg, and see how differently they turn out.

Making Faces

When you first began to scribble on paper, you probably started very soon to draw faces and learned to make them look happy or unhappy just by turning the mouth up or down. You discovered that there are lots of ways of having fun with faces. Maybe in October you make a head out of a pumpkin for Halloween and put a candle inside it. Perhaps you live where there's a lot of snow and you make a snowman—and give him a face with two stones for eyes and a carrot nose. You can draw faces in the sand with your finger. You can do the same in snow, dirt, or even salt! Perhaps the first face that anyone ever drew was just a line scratched on a rock between two marks that happened to look like eyes.

Try to remember what you drew after you started to draw faces. You probably added arms and legs—just lines sticking out from the face, a bit like Humpty Dumpty. But the face was the important part of the drawing—because faces are so important to us.

My Mum, by Tom Double, age 4 .

The Halloween jack-o'-lantern made by schoolchildren looks something like the kind of masked head or painted face that people have used for magic.

(Left) *Just the eyes and nose of this figure are enough to tell you that it's meant to be a human being. It's the same kind of idea as the child's drawing on the opposite page. But this is the image of an ancestor in West Africa, beautifully made of wood, brass, and copper.*

(Right) *The sculptor Norman Mommens made a series of little figures small enough to hold in your hand, with faces in the middle of the body. We always seem to look at faces first. Does it bother you that this one is in an odd place?*

This golden mask was made to cover the face of a great king when he was buried at Mycenae in Greece about 3,500 years ago. The archeologist who dug it up, Heinrich Schliemann, believed it had been made for King Agamemnon. But it was not made to look like Agamemnon or anyone else. It was the face of a king, but not any particular king.

Faces and Gods

Human faces and images are important in many of the religions of the world. In some religions it's forbidden to make images of people or animals, because it's thought that people might worship them instead of the god or gods they represent. In other religions, images are valued as a way to help people worship.

(Above) *This image of Jesus Christ is made of mosaic and is part of the ceiling of Monreale Cathedral in Italy. It shows him as Christ Pantocrator, which means "Christ, Ruler of All."*

The ancient Egyptians observed things very carefully. In this picture of the sculptor Ipuy and his wife, their clothes and jewelry are shown in wonderful detail. Even their cat (which wears a silver earring!) is shown, and its kitten. But we don't get any idea of what kind of people they were. That wasn't what the Egyptians were interested in doing in their art 3,500 years ago.

"Real-life" Faces

We're used to the idea of drawing or painting faces to look like a particular person. And we see faces in photographs all the time—in books, magazines, newspapers, and advertisements. But for a long time, artists weren't interested in making faces that showed character. Their job was to show what kind of person the face belonged to—usually a king, or a queen, or a general. The ancient Egyptians and

You might meet this young man out jogging, with his sweatband and his curly sideburns. He's a Greek charioteer, and the artist made this bronze figure of him about 2,500 years ago.

Chinese painted or carved people to show their position as rulers or officials, rather than show them as simply men and women.

The change came with the ancient Greeks. At first the statues made in the Greek city-states were very like those of the ancient Egyptians. But sometime between 2,500 and 2,600 years ago (we don't know exactly, since most of the statues have been lost), Greek artists started to make their stone statues look more like real human beings. Bodies became more natural-looking—and faces did, too. These ideas spread from the artists who carved in stone to the makers of bronze statues and the vase painters. Other people, including the ancient Romans, started to copy them.

The Egyptians painted portraits on the wooden covers in which mummies were placed. This girl must have died very young. With her large and beautiful eyes, her full mouth, and her head turned to one side, she shows very well how much the Egyptians had learned from the Greeks and Romans about making portraits "real." This one was painted about 1,900 years ago.

This doesn't mean, of course, that afterward artists only made faces that looked like they belonged to real people. But the idea had taken root that it was an interesting thing to do. So since that time it's been possible to look at a carving or a painting and think, "That man looks just like Mr. So-and-So who runs the pizza parlor on the corner." People

in paintings and sculpture had started to have what we call a "modern" face. Faces had begun to show their owners' characters.

This was true whether artists were drawing or painting imaginary faces or making pictures of real people—portraits.

This idea of showing people as they really are has produced some of the most

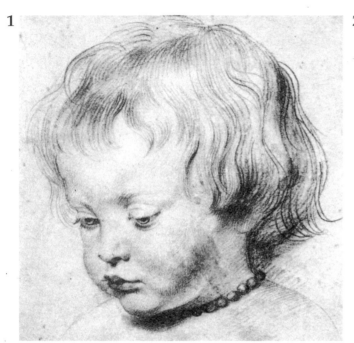

marvelous pictures that have been painted over the last 600 years. All sorts of faces—beautiful faces, ugly faces, sad faces, humorous faces, faces that move us and faces that we recognize. Look at the pictures on these two pages, and try making your own character study of each one. It's easy to imagine what kind of people they were. Try it the other way around, too. Think of a particular kind of person, perhaps a mean person or a very jolly person, and try drawing a picture of someone like that. Then ask your friends or family if they know what kind of a person you've drawn.

1. Peter Paul Rubens (1577–1640) was often asked to paint the portraits of important people. But this drawing of his son Nicholas is different. You feel how fond and proud he was of the boy.

2. Rembrandt Harmenszoon van Rijn (1606–1669) painted family faces all his life. You feel he caught his teenage son Titus exactly. Rembrandt's series of self-portraits, painted all through his life, are an extraordinary record of the changes in the way he painted.

3. The 13th-century artist who carved this figure of a German princess on the cathedral at Naumburg in Germany gave her an unforgettable smile. It's as if a press photographer caught a movie star at a premiere, clutching her cloak around her.

4. Here is the drawing that the German artist Albrecht Dürer (1471–1528) made of his mother. Her face is lined, her flesh is old, and she seems to have lost her teeth. You have the feeling you could meet her on the street today.

5. Here's a man who jumps out of the picture at you, he seems like such a real person. But we don't know who he is, or who painted him, just that he lived in the 15th century.

6. This young man was painted in Italy by one of the most famous painters of the 15th century, Sandro Botticelli. The youth's hand, with its swollen knuckles, looks arthritic (according to doctors who have looked at this picture).

5

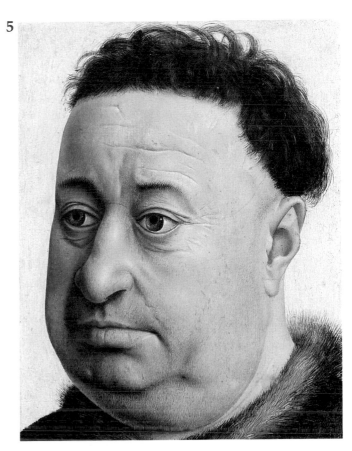

6

Having Your Portrait Painted

Some portraits were included in larger pictures. For example, in the Netherlands 500 years ago, it was the fashion for rich people to have a religious picture painted to go in a church. The artist often included portraits of the donors ("donor" means giver), as in the painting below.

There was no photography until about 150 years ago, so having your portrait painted was much more common then than it is today. For artists it was very good for business! Portraits were used in many of the ways we use photographs now—paintings of the children for their mother's birthday, a solemn painting of the board of directors of an institution to hang in the boardroom, a propaganda painting that made a ruler or a pope look powerful and splendid. If you were a prince you could order a portrait of the princess you were thinking of marrying, to see if you liked the look of her. (Princesses were unlikely to be allowed to do the same.)

The painting below, The Virgin and Child with Saints and Donors, is by the Flemish artist Hans Memling (about 1430–1494). It's a triptych (a picture made in three panels), and was commissioned by Sir John Donne of Kidwelly, Wales, in about 1477. It is quite small (the center wooden panel is only 28 by 26³/₄ inches, and the side panels 28 by 11³/₄ inches), so it was probably meant for use by Sir John's family, not to be displayed in a church. In the center panel, Sir John is on the left, under the protection of St. Catherine (standing behind him), and his wife, Elizabeth, is kneeling on the right, protected by St. Barbara, holding a tower (her "attribute"). The little girl on the right is probably their daughter, Anne. So in this picture there are three members of the family (almost as big as the saints). The side panels show St. John the Baptist (left) and St. John the Evangelist (right). Perhaps these saints were chosen because they shared the name of the donor, the person who commissioned the work.

Candles and Clues

One of the most unusual self-portraits you could find was painted by the Spanish artist Goya. He painted himself in his studio, holding his palette and his brushes and wearing his special "candleholder hat." His son Javier tells us that his father always painted during daylight, but since he knew that his pictures were often seen in the evening he liked to touch them up in the evening—by candlelight—to make sure they'd look their best. For this purpose he had a special hat made with pincers to hold candles.

The picture also gives us some other clues to Goya's way of painting. If you look carefully at his palette you can make out all the colors that he liked to put into his pictures and the different kinds of brushes he used. A friend reported that he used his finger and the tip of a knife as well.

Family Faces

The faces that an artist sees most are often those of his or her family. So it's not surprising that artists draw or paint their wives or husbands, their children, and their parents. (And members of the family usually model for free—unlike others!) The artists know them well, so these pictures are particularly interesting and often seem "true" in a special way.

The portraits that artists paint of themselves are special too. They sometimes use themselves as guinea pigs to try out new techniques. And it's interesting to find out how an artist sees himself or herself.

Faces That Tell Their Feelings

Once artists had become interested in showing people as they really were, they started to be interested in showing feelings.

About 300 years ago, faces in pictures and sculptures started to show feelings more obviously. Suffering saints rolled their eyes up to heaven. People laughed in pictures, and mothers looked lovingly at their babies.

Artists in the 20th century have tried out a variety of ways of showing feelings in their paintings. They don't always show faces the way they are. They sometimes show "more feeling than face." Think of a person's head—eyes, eyebrows, nose, cheeks, mouth, chin, ears, hair. Take a couple of these features and experiment with them. Try drawing them in different ways to look frightened, surprised, happy, or sad. Now go through the whole of this book just looking at one feature in all the faces—say the eyes—and see what you can discover about the ways artists show people's feelings.

Ian Morton, age 12, seems to have caught the character of his school friend amazingly well. How do you think he did it?

William Hogarth (1697–1764), who painted this picture, The Shrimp Girl, *described her as "a blooming young girl of fifteen." She's so fresh and cheerful that you smile when you look at her.*

Picasso, who painted this picture, called it Weeping Woman. *He painted a number of pictures with this title, trying out different ways of showing sadness and suffering.*

Evelyn (age 10), who did this pen drawing, called it Crying Face. *How has she shown the girl's sadness?*

From Miniature to Mural

You might see the pictures you've just been looking at inside a house or a school or a church, in a museum or an art gallery. But pictures of people come in all sizes. The smallest are only one or two inches high. These tiny pictures, called miniatures, were made to be carried around, sometimes on a chain around your neck, to remind you of your loved ones. It was a lot like putting a photo of someone in your wallet. Miniature painters also made tiny portraits of kings and queens and other famous people. These are often a very good record of what these people really looked like. Miniatures were particularly popular at the time of Queen Elizabeth I.

At the other end of the scale you'll find people's faces, several yards high, outside. The ones you notice most are probably advertisements or posters, but you may also sometimes find paintings of people on walls, like the one below of the South African leader Nelson Mandela, by the black South African artist known as Dumile. (His full name was Mhlabi Zwelidumile Mxgazi, but that was a mouthful!) He painted this mural on a wall in New York.

This miniature shows the poet Henry Percy, the ninth Earl of Northampton. The artist was the famous miniature painter Nicholas Hilliard (1547–1619), who painted this piece about 400 years ago. It's a little larger (2 inches high) than this photograph.

Dumile (1939–1991) stands beside his mural of Nelson Mandela on the Pathfinder Building in New York City.

6 • Body Language

Think of someone you know. You probably think first of the face. But bodies are important too, and often are as interesting and expressive as faces. You can recognize people from a distance by the way they walk or run, sit or hold their head. Your body is a part of your character, just as your face is.

For artists, bodies have meant different things at different times. And they have thought in different ways about how to show them. The ancient Egyptians, for example, showed what they *knew* the different parts of the body were like, rather than what they actually *saw* when they looked at a body. You read in the last chapter about the ancient Greeks making sculptures that looked like real people. Of course, that meant their entire bodies, not just their heads and faces.

In some pictures and sculptures, size is the important thing. The artist may show God much bigger than the surrounding saints. An important ruler may be shown much bigger than his wife or children. Or an artist may make one part of the body bigger than the rest because it's particularly important for some reason—for example, a hand giving a blessing. Artists who draw caricatures (pictures that exaggerate particular features of people) always pick one or more parts of the body to make you see the person in a certain way—to make him or her look funny, or greedy, or stupid . . .

The stone carving on the opposite page is of an Egyptian grain official and his family. It was made about 4,350 years ago. He was an important man—and was considered much more important than his wife (kneeling on the right) and daughter (on the left), so they were shown as tiny figures just coming up to his knees. The statue is 22$\frac{1}{2}$ inches high.

Here—above and on the opposite page—are two works of art that are interesting to look at together. They both show people (or one person) in bed, but they do it in very different ways. The carving above is from a church in France and was made about 800 years ago. It shows the three kings of the Bible story, the wise men, being told in a dream by an angel not to go back to King Herod to tell him where to find the baby Jesus, but to go home another way. The artist wanted to show all three kings, so he carved them one on top of the other, as if seen from above. He did the same with the cover on the bed. But we see the angel from the side. The three kings wear their crowns even in bed, so that we know they're kings. The angel touches one king's arm and points, as if to say, "Wake up and be on your way!" The scene is not at all realistic or natural, but we can easily understand what's going on here.

sleeping child· covered with blanket.

Henry Moore (1898–1987), one
of the most famous sculptors of
the 20th century, was a war
artist in World War II, employed
by the British government. He
filled a whole sketchbook with
drawings of people taking shelter
in the Underground (the
subway) from the German
bombing of London. Families
slept there at night. In this
drawing he shows a sleeping
child. Like one of the three kings
in the stone carving, the child
has his arm outside the blanket.
But how different the scene is.
Moore shows the child's body by
the way he draws the blanket
humped over it. The child looks
as if he really is asleep—eyes
closed and arm hanging limply
down. He looks like any child
today would look asleep in bed.

Bodies in Movement

Artists have a whole range of ways of showing bodies in movement. On the Mediterranean island of Crete about 3,500 years ago, the people who lived there, the Minoans, made "action" carvings out of ivory, like the bull leaper below. The artist wasn't concerned about the bone structure or the muscles, but wanted to give the feeling of the way the young men (and sometimes girls) leaped over the bulls, flying through the air.

   Sports of all kinds have given artists interesting opportunities to show figures in movement. Over 3,000 years separate the carver of the Minoan acrobat from three well-known artists in the 19th and 20th centuries who enjoyed studying, modeling, drawing, and painting acrobats and other circus performers. Edgar Degas (1834–1917), Henri de Toulouse-Lautrec (1864–1901), and Marc Chagall (1887–1985) all painted in France. The first two were regular visitors to the famous Cirque Fernando in Paris. They were different artists with different interests, so the way they portrayed the bodies of the performers naturally was different. Look at the pictures before reading the captions, and see if you can figure out what interested each artist.

Chagall took a number of figures from the circus and put them together in a composition that gives us the feeling of being at the circus, but is not like any real circus. Whoever heard of an acrobat balancing on a violin? Chagall often put a violin in his pictures—perhaps he was thinking of his violin lessons as a boy.

A Minoan bull leaper carved out of ivory, from Knossos, Crete.

Degas painted the famous woman acrobat La La hanging by her teeth from a rope high up at the Cirque Fernando in Paris in 1879. Imagine the painting without the background of the circus building. Would the figure be more dramatic or less? Would you be able to tell that La La was hanging high up? How did Degas show where the lights in the circus are?

58

Find other pairs of pictures, of dancers perhaps, or skaters, and try to guess what it was that most interested each artist. Was it the shape the body makes when doing a particular action? Was it the color? Was it the background? Was it the pattern the figures make? Sometimes it's easier to tell if you hold the picture upside down. Try it.

Skaters' bodies make marvelous shapes. The canals of the Netherlands freeze over in winter, so skating is a popular sport there, and was a favorite subject for Dutch artists in the 17th century. The Scottish lochs (lakes) also sometimes freeze. In 1784 there was a very cold winter in Scotland and everyone went skating, including the Reverend Robert Walker, on Duddingston Loch near Edinburgh. The Scottish portrait painter, Sir Henry Raeburn (1756–1823), saw what a wonderful shape the minister made in his black clothes.

(Right) *Tracy Beresford painted this picture,* Happy Skaters, *for a competition when she was a child. She was more interested in color than shape. She captured the feeling of balancing with your arms and the sense of fun very well.*

(Left) *This bronze statue of a girl running was made in Tuscany, Italy, about 2,500 years ago. (It's only 5¹/₈ inches high.) Why do you think she's holding her arms out? And why did the artist give her wings on her feet? Could you imagine a modern girl in a miniskirt looking like this?*

(Right) *This 20th-century figure has the same shape as the running girl. Guess what kind of a sportsman it is. It's Picasso's idea of a soccer player! He cut the shape out of metal, bent it, and painted it. (It's 21 inches high.) What do you think he thought was most important about soccer players?*

Alphabet Bodies

You can fit bodies into all sorts of shapes—even into letters of the alphabet. This young artist, Frances Campbell, made an alphabet out of the bodies of boatmen and their poles. (C, A, and M are the first three letters of "Cambridge"—Cambridge, England, that is, where Frances lives). You could try making letters out of the bodies of football players, dancers, skiers . . .

Another way of showing a body in motion was used by the
makers of Indian religious figures. When they made a figure
of a god dancing, they showed him with *two* pairs of arms,
each arm in a different position. It's almost as if the arms were
actually moving.

This is a 16th-century figure
from South India. It is of the
Hindu god Nataraja dancing.
His hair is flying out to show
that he is whirling around. In
his back left hand he holds fire
(meaning destruction). His
front right hand is in a position
that means "Fear not." The
figure is 36 inches high, and
made of copper.

Bodies at Work

Another way of showing figures in movement is to show people working. The ancient Greek artists who decorated vases showed dancers and sportsmen, women weaving, and sculptors at work. The ancient Egyptians made small clay figures of people doing a variety of jobs—sometimes they buried these figures in tombs. The Romans showed people like butchers and bakers in the panels they carved out of stone. And artists in the Middle Ages who illustrated the Books of Hours (religious books) included scenes of country people at work—plowing, harvesting hay, shearing sheep, pruning vines.

We not only enjoy these models and paintings as works of art, but we also learn a lot from them about the way people lived, what they looked like, and what clothes they wore.

The same 19th-century artists who were interested in acrobats and dancers found people at work good to paint too—people gardening, breaking stones, hanging out the wash, ironing . . .

The Japanese artist Hokusai (1760–1849) was well known for his drawings and prints of people. He made sheets of drawings of people at play and at work—like this peasant carrying a heavy sack of grain.

Vincent van Gogh (1853–1890) went to work as a preacher among the miners in a poor area of Belgium. It was there he drew these women miners carrying sacks of coal on their heads.

This is the illumination for the month of October from the Book of Hours, Les Très Riches Heures du Duc de Berry. *The Duc de Berry was a great patron of the arts in 15th-century France. He commissioned the illustrations for this book from the Limbourg brothers, three well-known young artists who worked together on illuminations (and who all died before they were 30).*

The scene is just outside Paris. In the background is the palace of the Louvre (as it then was). The man in red is riding a horse, which is drawing a harrow to break up the ground. The one in blue carries a sling full of seed and is sowing it by hand. The figure in the middle is not an archer practicing, but a scarecrow!

The artist shows the men's bodies moving naturally as they go about their tasks. But there are other interesting "natural" points about this picture. Look at the figures again. You'll see that they cast shadows, even the tiny figures in the background, and that the boat on the river is reflected in the water. Nothing special about that, you may think. But this small picture (almost the same size as on this page) is the oldest example we know of an artist showing shadows and reflections. It was the start of looking at light in a different way, of showing the world in a more "natural" way.

Pairs and Groups

Once an artist includes more than one figure in a drawing or painting, or groups figures together in a sculpture, he or she can try out all sorts of new ideas. The artist can make the figures connect or contrast with each other, and can make things happen between them. Think for example of the figures of a mother and her child, a favorite subject for artists. (The most popular pair of figures in European art is the Virgin, often called the Madonna, and Child, because so much of the art of the Western world has to do with the Christian religion.) If you think of the different ways in which mothers hold their babies, you can imagine the enormous variety of paintings and sculptures on this theme. Because Jesus was no ordinary baby, European artists have wanted to show the special quality of this child, and the special relationship between him and his mother.

The mother-and-child pair also appears in many paintings that have nothing to do with religion. Mary Cassatt (1844–1926) was an American painter and printmaker who worked mostly in Paris. She admired the work of Degas very much. She first saw one of his paintings in the window of a picture dealer. "I used to go and flatten my nose against that window and absorb all I could of his art," she said once. "It changed my life." She loved painting mothers and children. The Boating Party *(right) is a mother-and-child pair, but it's much more than that. The shapes of the boatman, of the sail, and of the boat itself are very important parts of the picture. Try to imagine what the picture would be like without them. Now imagine the mother and child in clothes like those in the picture below the Cassatt. Would the picture then look like a Madonna and Child? If not, why not?*

(Left) The sculptor who carved these figures of the Madonna and Child out of stone lived in Lombardy, in the north of Italy, in the 12th century. For him, it seems, the important thing is the tenderness between the two. They could be almost any mother and child. (The statue is 29 inches high.)

Andrea Mantegna (1431–1506)
was the son of a carpenter and
lived in the north of Italy. This
gifted boy was adopted by his
teacher so that he could use
Andrea's talents without
paying him.

Mantegna painted six Virgin
and Child pictures. In this one
on the left, the shapes of the
mother and child fit into each
other perfectly. They are bound
together not only by the child's
sleeping head, which is cupped
by its mother's hand into the
hollow of her neck and wrapped
around by her veil, but also by
the feeling of closeness that they
give. Like the carving from
Lombardy, these are religious
figures, but could also be any
mother and child. The picture is
painted in distemper on canvas
and is 16½ by 12½ inches.

65

Before radio and television, cassette, and CD players, people had to make their own music. They made music in their homes, in church, and in concerts. People singing and playing instruments together made an interesting and popular subject for artists.

Here are two works of art, each made in Italy at the time of the Renaissance. The group of child singers, carved out of marble by Luca della Robbia (1400–1482), is part of a larger marble frieze of angels and children singing, dancing, and making music. Della Robbia made it for the cathedral in Florence. (Today it's in the cathedral museum.) The boys are all reading the words out of the same book, so they have to lean over each other's shoulders to see it. Della Robbia used this opportunity to link them in an unusual way, overlapping them and using their arms to lead your eye from one body to the next.

Lorenzo Costa (about 1460–1535) painted two young men and a girl singing to the accompaniment of a lute. He painted them standing very close together—the girl has her hand on the lute player's shoulder. This gives you the feeling that they must be singing in close harmony. Look at their eyes. They're all looking in different directions. Why do you think they're doing that? Which way do you look when you're singing (without a conductor)? Would this group look out of place around a microphone today?

Clothes Carry Messages

It's easy to recognize a policewoman or a firefighter, a nurse or a Boy Scout—you recognize them by their clothes, their uniforms. At a football or baseball game, you can recognize the fans of the two teams by the caps or jackets they wear. In the same way, some people's clothes carry more general messages. "I'm wearing designer jeans—so I'm fashionable." Or "I'm wearing the So-and-So school logo—so I'm with the 'in' crowd."

Clothes in art carry messages too. You can recognize a Japanese samurai (warrior) by his clothes and his swords, a Roman emperor by his special toga. The various religious orders of monks and nuns in the Middle Ages and the Renaissance wore particular habits—for example, the Franciscans wore brown, the Dominicans black and white.

Clothes in portraits often carry messages about wealth and power. You can see this very clearly in portraits painted at the time of Henry VIII and Elizabeth I. The clothes are made of precious silks embroidered with jewels, and are often padded to make the wearer look larger and more powerful. We sometimes talk about "power dressing" today, and although the styles are different we mean the same kind of thing.

(Below left) *This picture by the German artist Hans Holbein the Younger (about 1497–1543) is called* The Ambassadors, *because it shows Jean de Dinteville (on the left), who was the French ambassador to England at the age of only 29, and his ambassador friend Bishop Georges de Selve (only 25), who had come to visit him in London. The French ambassador is a perfect example of power dressing—enormous padded shoulders, silk tunic, fur-trimmed coat, and gold chain of office around his neck.*

The picture is interesting for a number of other reasons. There are a lot of instruments in it—for example, globes, sundials, and quadrants. There is also a lute and a case of flutes, a hymn book, and an arithmetic book. Perhaps they are there to show the wide range of interests of these two men.

But what is that strange diagonal shape on the floor? You can find the answer by lifting up this book (open at this page), holding it level with your eyes, and looking at the shape in the picture from that position. You should see something that reminds you of death. Holbein may have meant it to remind us that, however powerful we are, and however much knowledge we have, we all have to die in the end. So in this picture it's not just the clothes that carry a message but the objects as well. This is a large picture, nearly 7 feet square, and was painted by Holbein in 1532.

7 • Decoration

To keep yourself warm, keep out drafts, and have something to hold your food and drink, you need very little. Some straw, a sack, a leaf, a hollow gourd will do. So why have people spent so much time, energy, and money making things that have to do with everyday life so complicated—and sometimes so beautiful? There's no simple answer. The wish to make our surroundings more interesting and beautiful than they need to be is one of the things that make humans different from animals.

It would be hard to guess what the object below left is for. It's an ancient Egyptian covered spoon for holding cosmetics, in the form of a girl being towed through the water by a gazelle. It's 9 inches long and was made about 2,400 years ago, from alabaster (a kind of stone) and slate.

Next to Your Skin

We start with our bodies. When we use makeup, or style our hair, we're doing what people have been doing for thousands of years. The ways in which men and women have decorated their bodies have taken different forms at different times.

Women often wear eye makeup today, just as the women of ancient Egypt did. Hindu women wear a red dot, the *tilak*, on their forehead—both as a decoration and as a religious sign (the footprint of a god). As soon as people started using cosmetics, they needed small boxes to hold powders and ointments. And then they began to decorate their boxes. You only have to look along the shelves of any cosmetic department in a big store today to realize that people like to have their cosmetics and perfumes attractively packaged.

Compare the hairstyles of the men who lived about 2,300 years ago (page 25), 500 years ago (page 49), and 200 years ago (page 20), with the punk hairstyles of the modern couple in this photograph.

You can see how differently men have arranged their hair over the ages. Remember that what one person thinks is beautiful, another person—perhaps in a different part of the world— thinks is ugly.

Jewelry

Ornamenting the human body is perhaps the oldest art there is. Wearing jewelry is one of the main ways men and women make themselves look beautiful. Jewelry can be made of gold or plastic, silver or ceramic, and include precious gemstones, or not-so-precious amber, pebbles, or beads.

Jewelry also carries messages, as clothes do. Probably the best-known piece of "message" jewelry is the wedding ring. But rings carry all sorts of other messages—an engagement ring, a mourning ring (which people used to wear when someone close to them died), a friendship ring, and the pope's ring (which is handed on from one pope to the next). Crowns, necklaces, bracelets, anklets, earrings, nose rings, and brooches can all tell us something about the person wearing them. The more precious the materials from which the jewelry is made, the more important—or richer—the person is likely to be.

This is a torque, which is a piece of jewelry once worn around the neck by a chieftain or a king. This one is made of a mixture of silver and gold called electrum. It's 7¾ inches across and was dug up in the east of England. It's about 2,000 years old. Other torques made of electrum, gold, or bronze have been found in Switzerland, Germany, France, Belgium, and Ireland.

The ancient Egyptians used gold and gemstones such as amethyst, garnet, and especially turquoise. Sometimes they were made into "message" jewelry for a ruler to wear. Often jewelry was buried to go with the ruler into the next life.

The ancient Greeks also were very skilled at making jewelry. Later on, in the Middle Ages, jewelers used their craft mainly for religious objects—Christian crucifixes (crosses) or boxes for holding relics of saints (bones, for example), and crowns for kings, queens, and emperors. People in Central and South America often used silver and gold, since there was a lot to be found in countries such as Mexico and Peru. Much of the jewelry made in Europe from the 16th century onward was made out of the gold and silver that the Spanish and Portuguese took from Central and South America.

Badges, Patches, and Emblems

Most people collect something at some time in their life. What do *you* collect? Maybe old bottles, stamps, or postcards. Or patches and stickers? Collecting patches, or badges, goes back a long way. In the Middle Ages, you wouldn't have gone on vacation (vacations are a modern invention), but you might have gone on a pilgrimage to a holy place. In Europe, many Christians made a pilgrimage to the church of St. James of Compostela, in Spain, just over the border from France. Pilgrim routes lead from all over Europe to Compostela. (You can still walk on some of them.) The emblem of St. James was a shell. Large numbers of badges were made, usually of tin, in the form of a shell and sold to pilgrims. They were just like tourist souvenirs.

Some of these badges were very beautifully made, like miniature sculptures. Those for pilgrims to Canterbury, England, to the shrine of St. Thomas à Becket, often show St. Thomas riding on horseback, or sailing back from exile in a boat. The sun was often included in pilgrim badges—not because it had anything to do with the saints, but because it was a sign left over from an earlier time when people had worshiped the sun.

The pilgrim badge above (measuring 3 1/4 inches across) is from the 14th century. It shows the head of St. Thomas à Becket inside a sun. The one below shows a sun inside a moon.

A 20th-century pilgrim badge!

Horse Brasses

Not only people have badges, but animals and machines do too. Anything for an excuse to decorate, it seems! Before vans and trucks took over, city streets were full of horse-drawn carts delivering things. In the country, all the machines and farm carts were drawn by horses, not tractors. People were proud of their big, strong cart-horses, and decorated their leather harnesses with polished brass disks, called horse brasses. About 3,000 different designs have been found, but they're nearly all based on three patterns: the crescent, the heart, and the sun. The horse always wore one with the sun design on its forehead. The original idea was to protect the horse and its driver from the evil eye. It's interesting to compare horse brasses with pilgrim badges. The designs are often quite similar, and you'll notice that the sun is used for both. The sun is still used to decorate many of the things that we use today.

Below is a horse brass based on the sun.

Diamonds and Hearts, Roses and Leaves

All around the world, people decorate the things they make with patterns. These may be geometric—an X, a zigzag, or a diamond—or represent a flower, perhaps a rose, or a leaf, a tree, or a heart.

The objects that people decorate are made of many different materials. All sorts of people whose work depends on daylight, the weather, or the seasons have traditionally made and decorated objects in their spare time. Shepherds, for example, often work with wood, passing the hours spent watching their sheep by carving sticks and shepherds' crooks, and making little boxes for their sweethearts. In America, Europe, and parts of Africa and Asia, people made beautiful wedding chests. Often the same kinds of decoration, of flowers and leaves, birds and fishes, are painted or carved on wedding chests from different parts of the world. The quilt shown on this page uses similar patterns. The men and women who designed quilts like these a hundred years ago created complicated arrangements of rosettes, suns and stars, leaves, feathers, chains, and diamonds.

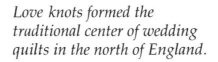

Love knots formed the traditional center of wedding quilts in the north of England.

The man who made this box for his beloved carved his name and the date into the design of rosettes, heart, and love knot.

Part of a quilt made by Elizabeth Sanderson (1861– 1934) in the north of England. See how many different motifs you can find.

What Do *You* Think?

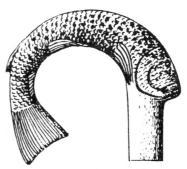

This shepherd's crook in the form of a fish is made from a sheep's horn, and the duck's head below is the top of a walking stick carved out of wood.

Is it more fun to have a walking stick with a duck handle than a plain one? Is it more interesting to have a brass door-knocker in the shape of a dolphin, a boat with a figurehead in the form of a mermaid?

Not everyone likes the idea of decoration. Religious sects such as the Quakers and the Shakers thought everything should be plain, with no decoration.

What do *you* think? If you like the idea of decoration, which of your possessions would you like to see decorated?

Around the House

Where there's no refrigerator or running water in a house, containers for storing foods and liquids are very important. They have to do their job efficiently—they must not leak, they must keep their contents clean and cool, and they must keep out animals and insects.

10,000 Years of Pots

Clay pots have been doing this job very well for the last 10,000 years. The word "pottery" covers both the simplest and plainest terra-cotta (baked earth) pots for everyday use and the finest "art" pots, meant more for looking at than using. The oldest pottery was made by modeling the pot from a lump of clay, or building it up from a coil of clay (like a long sausage). About 4,500 years ago the pottery wheel, more or less as we know it today, was invented. (You put the clay on a revolving disk and form it with both hands.) That made it possible for potters to produce many more pots much more quickly—and in more

We probably all use pottery in some form or other every day of our lives. Here's a child's plate and mug from Germany. Roosters and hens keep popping up in the decoration of all sorts of things, from weathervanes to chests, from toys to textiles.

regular shapes. About a thousand years later, potters began to use glaze (a hard coating that was baked onto the pot), which made the pots waterproof, and so better for storage.

The peoples around the Mediterranean Sea needed to store such items as water, wine, and olive oil, so many of their pots are designed to hold these liquids. Potters experimented from earliest times with different forms of decoration. Simple scratched lines developed into geometric patterns. First there were primitive drawings of animals, and later more realistic pictures.

The native peoples of Central and South America have a long and interesting tradition of pottery for everyday use. They often made their pots with geometric patterns cut into them or painted on them.

This pot, made in Crete about 3,400 years ago, is a pilgrim flask. (It's 11 inches high.) You can imagine a hot and weary pilgrim trekking to some distant shrine, gratefully taking a swig from it (like a hiker today drinking from a plastic water bottle). There were lots of octopuses in the sea around Crete, so it was natural for the potter to use one as his decoration. The octopus suits the shape of the pot marvelously.

On this page you can see just a few of the many Botswana basket patterns and their names.

Forehead of the zebra

Running ostrich

100,000 Years of Baskets

Clay is not the only cheap material around for making storage containers. In many places—particularly Central and South America, Africa, and Asia—people use grasses, reeds, cane, bamboo, and bark for making baskets. We tend to think of baskets as something to take along to the beach or for holding laundry. But baskets have a hundred other uses. They can be used for shopping, for drying food in the sun or for storing it, or for carrying a meal (like a lunch box). Baskets are used as traps for catching fish and birds, and as cages for carrying animals and songbirds. They can be used for storing clothes.

There are two ways of making baskets. You can either weave them or coil them. In almost every village in Africa, you can find many ordinary people skilled at making baskets. Their sizes and shapes are as varied as their uses. In Nigeria, there are as many as 30 different types of rectangular baskets. The traditional patterns are just as varied as the shapes, often geometric. Zulu patterns are made up of lines, triangles, and diamonds, and Botswana ones are often circular patterns.

Ribs of the giraffe

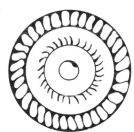

Roof of the rondvel (hut)

A selection of Botswana baskets made from palm fiber. The different colors of the fiber are used to create a variety of patterns.

Flight of the swallow

Cellini's Saltcellar to End All Saltcellars!

Benvenuto Cellini (1500–1571) came from Florence and was both a sculptor and a goldsmith. He kept a journal, which still exists, and so we know a lot about him. He gives a very vivid picture of life in a goldsmith's workshop in Rome—his commissions for jewelry from flirtatious noble ladies and from Pope Clement VII, his rivalry with other goldsmiths, his friends.

Cellini designed this extraordinary gold saltcellar (a dish for salt) for Francis I (the same King of France for whom Leonardo da Vinci worked). He must have been very pleased at the king's reaction to it: *"When I showed it to his Majesty, he gave a great cry of astonishment, and could not take his eyes off it."*

Then the king did something nice: *"He told me to take it back to my house, saying that he would tell me at the proper time what I should do with it. So I carried it home and sent at once to invite several of my best friends. We had a jolly dinner together, placing the saltcellar in the middle of the table, and so we were the first to use it."*

Cellini describes his saltcellar (13 inches wide and 10½ inches high): *"The Sea* [shown in the form of the sea-god Neptune] *carried a trident in his right hand and in his left I put a ship of delicate workmanship to hold the salt. Below him were his four sea-horses, fashioned like our horses from the head to the front hoofs; all the rest of their body resembled a fish . . . I had portrayed Earth in the form of a very handsome woman, holding her horn of plenty. By her right hand I placed a little temple, most delicately wrought, to contain the pepper."*

Jacks of All Trades—and Masters of All

As well as making and decorating things to use from cheap materials, people have also wanted to surround themselves with objects made out of precious materials, such as silver and gold. There is a tradition in some parts of the world of making very fine objects to be used on the dinner tables of wealthy people. This is the work of silversmiths and goldsmiths.

Today we usually think of painters only painting pictures, of sculptors only making sculptures, of potters only making pots, of silversmiths only making silver objects, and so on. Most artists specialize. But it hasn't always been that way. For example, during the Renaissance many artists were eager to take on commissions from patrons for different kinds of work. Well-known artists did not consider it beneath them to design coins, medals, jewelry, furniture, or fountains. There were painters who were also sculptors, sculptors who were also architects, and so on. The most extraordinary example of this is Leonardo da Vinci (1452–1519), who came from Florence and worked for noble patrons in both Italy and France. He was a painter, sculptor, architect, military engineer, *and* mathematician! He also invented things (including a primitive airplane) and wrote about both scientific matters and painting.

Another famous artist of the Renaissance, Michelangelo (1475–1564), who was a painter, sculptor, and architect, also made designs for the decoration of his buildings, while Raphael (1483–1520) was well known in his lifetime for his paintings and his decoration designs.

A

B

*On his way to France in 1537, Cellini stayed with Cardinal Bembo, a famous scholar and poet, and he designed this portait medal of his friend. Cellini tells us in his journal that he spent 200 hours on the wax model of the portrait (**A**), but only 3 hours on the winged horse Pegasus (**B**) for the other side of the medal. Bembo was puzzled: "This horse seems to me ten times more difficult to do than this little portrait on which you have bestowed so much pains. I cannot understand what made it such a labor." But he liked it, and gave Cellini 3 horses in return.*

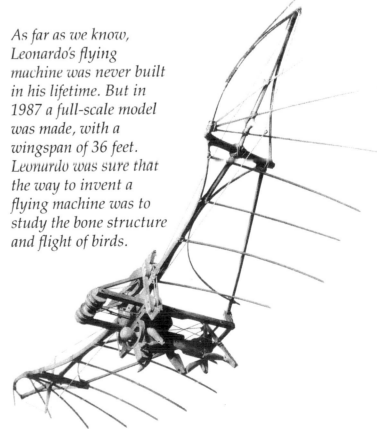

As far as we know, Leonardo's flying machine was never built in his lifetime. But in 1987 a full-scale model was made, with a wingspan of 36 feet. Leonardo was sure that the way to invent a flying machine was to study the bone structure and flight of birds.

Decorating Floors and Walls

Your house may be built of brick, stone, concrete, wood—or a mixture of these. The roof could be of tile, slate, or wood. But there are many kinds of dwellings in the world that are made in very different ways.

Rugs on the Move

People who are nomadic (who move from place to place with their herds of animals) live in tents or lightweight dwellings, so that they can easily take them down, carry them, and put

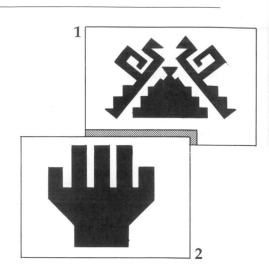

These Afghans are wrapping a kilim around the frame of their traditional yurt (tent).

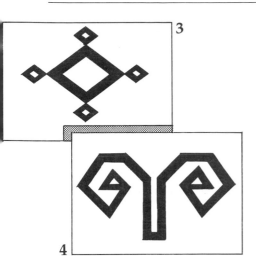

(Left) *Some examples of kilim patterns:*
(**1**) *birds*
(**2**) *hand*
(**3**) *eye*
(**4**) *ram's horns.*

A Kurdish bag.

them up again somewhere else. Some nomadic peoples, in Iran and Afghanistan for example, use long strips of woven cloth to cover the frames of their tents. They make rugs for the floor and weave saddlebags to carry their belongings on horseback. They don't own many things, so they make the most of their kilims (rugs and hangings) by using natural dyes and by weaving them in rich colors in a variety of patterns.

You see the same patterns in kilims (geometric patterns, the Tree of Life, eyes, hands, birds, animals) that you find in folk art in many different parts of the world. In this book, how many things have birds as part of their decoration?

This Flemish tapestry, made in about 1500, shows The Unicorn in Captivity, *a scene from the series* The Hunt of the Unicorn. *Stories of this imaginary creature, a horse with a single horn, were a popular subject in art.*

Tapestries on the Wall

In the Middle Ages, the palaces of the rich must have been pretty cold and uncomfortable, with their stone walls and floors. People hung woven tapestries over their walls, both to make the rooms warmer and to decorate them. Many of these tapestries are works of art, with beautiful pictures of flowers, animals, and people. Some come in a series, so that the artist could illustrate a story in several installments around a room (like a painted fresco).

In the 20th century, artists have taken up tapestry again—but not for practical use. The French artist Jean Lurçat (1892–1966) designed a remarkable series of tapestries that now hangs in the town of Angers, France. It's called The Song of the World, and it tells the story of man from the creation to the nuclear age. Lurçat called this part of it Man in Glory, at Peace. Remember the other images in this book, and try to figure out the meaning here of the sun, the stars, the owl, the tree, the leaves, and the hands.

Tiles, Patterns, and Pictures

You can find tiles in schools and stores, bathrooms and banks, fireplaces and fishmarkets. You may also find them in mosques, churches, kitchens, subway or bus stations, restaurants, and town halls—anywhere where it's useful to have a hard surface that's easy to clean. The word "tile" comes from the Latin word *tegula*, which means "cover." And that's just what tiles do very well—provide a cover for walls, floors, roofs, and even whole buildings. Tiles are made of pottery and are easy to decorate.

This is part of a panel of tiles showing how tiles were produced in the 18th century.
1.& 2. *Two workers are making tiles, using a tile frame.*
3. *A boy is shoveling away the leftover clay.*
4. *A man is stacking the half-dried tiles.*
5. *A worker is trimming the tiles.*
6. *A dog is asleep on the floor!*

Whatever you put in the corner of a tile will join up with the corners of the tiles next to it to form what is called a "link" pattern or design. The shape in the corner of these 17th-century Dutch bird tiles is called an ox-head design.

Dutch potters learned about tile-making from the Spaniards, and since the 17th century there has been an important tile industry in the Netherlands that still goes on today.

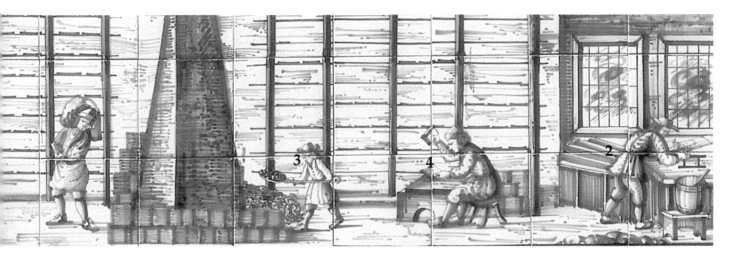

Tiles go back a long way—to the ancient Egyptians (as so many other things do). The Egyptians used blue glazed bricks (like tiles) to decorate their houses, and they also used them for making pictures.

Tiles have to be made in shapes that fit together to cover large areas of floors or walls. Most tiles nowadays are square, but it's also possible to make them in other shapes, such as rectangles and stars. The interesting thing about designing tiles is that you can make a mini-pattern on each tile, which then becomes part of a much larger pattern when you put several tiles together.

Some of the most interesting and beautiful tiles are found in those parts of the world where Islam is (or has been) an important religion—Iran (Persia), North Africa, Spain, and Portugal, for example. These are hot countries; cool, tiled surfaces are suitable here. (The same is true of mosaic—small pieces of glass or ceramic stuck together to form a hard covering for floors and walls.) The tiles are decorated with patterns, both geometric and flowers and leaves, and with birds. (In Islam it is forbidden to show people in art.)

This blue-and-white tile, which shows a peacock, was made in Syria around 1425.

Games, Toys, and Amusements

If you watch very young children playing, you'll notice that some of their favorite toys are the plainest and simplest—wooden spoons, empty boxes, bricks. It's adults who like to decorate games and toys (like everything else). From the time of the ancient Egyptians to our own day, we've had a colorful tradition of carved and painted toys and games. Some of them are very simple, like the whistling pottery roosters you find from Scandinavia to Mexico.

A pottery folk-art rooster from Finland. It whistles when you blow into its tail.

Some items are very beautiful, like the chess pieces you find in all sorts of different styles in, for example, India (where the game of chess came from originally), China, Japan, Italy, Spain, and Scotland. Other toys have complicated machinery and were quite high-tech in their time, like the mechanical silver swan shown below that bends its neck and appears to gobble up silver fishes, to the accompaniment of its own music.

Today's cheap toys are sometimes tomorrow's valued antiques. There are still markets and fairs in some European countries, and in Africa and Asia, where you can buy traditional toys and ornaments. It can be fun to wonder which modern toys, amusements, and ornaments will be valued by people in a hundred years' time. Try it with a friend, and see how your lists compare.

A silver swan automaton, made in the English workshop of James Cox in about 1773. It still works!

This bishop was among the 78 chess pieces discovered on the Isle of Lewis off the Scottish coast in 1831. They're beautifully carved out of ivory and have Celtic decorations, and are probably about 800 years old. (They're the same size as in this picture.)

This large automaton is called **Tipu's Tiger.** *It shows a fierce wooden tiger (about life size) eating a European man. Tipu was an Indian ruler who hated the British and loved tigers. If you turn the handle in the tiger's side, air is pumped through a bellows to produce growls and cries, and the man moves his arm up and down.*

8 • Making Art

Have you ever worked as part of a group of people painting a mural, or making a collage or a collection of puppets? If so, you will have some idea of how artists worked in the past.

Workshops

The beautiful gold objects that have been found in the tombs of ancient Egypt were made in workshops. The stone figures of saints and prophets that you see on the front of medieval cathedrals, the marble friezes that the Romans carved, and the large fresco paintings of Renaissance Italy were all made by teams of people. There was always someone who made the plan—the owner of the workshop, the master builder, or the leader of the team. There was also a whole group of craftspeople, some very skilled, some still learning, who worked with the master. Those still learning, the apprentices, worked on the first stages: hewing out rough figures from blocks of stone, preparing wooden panels for painting, putting the first coat of plaster on a wall ready for a fresco painting. That way they learned a lot about materials and techniques. Cellini's saltcellar was designed by him (see page 74), but we know from his journal that much of the detailed work was done by goldsmiths under his direction.

Working Together

In the 20th century too there are many examples of people working as a team on a piece of art. In 1966 a group of artists decided for fun to make the longest drawing in the world—to stretch from London to Amsterdam! The drawing went over sidewalks and up walls, into a taxicab, over the taxi driver himself, through Heathrow airport, into a plane, out again at Schiphol airport, by bus into Amsterdam, along the streets, and finally it disappeared into a gutter outside the Stedelijk Museum. Paul Klee once said drawing was "taking a line for a walk"—these artists were certainly doing that!

This was a great day for a thousand English schoolchildren and their parents. They made big puppets to act out a folk story about the trickster Anansi. They made Anansi, his mother, some animals, and, biggest of all, the great sky god out of old baby buggy wheels, old clothes and boots, wicker, leftover cloth, a knapsack frame, paper, and plastic bottles.

Using Assistants

Even with single pictures, often more than one person worked on the same painting. With a portrait, for example, the master might sketch out the whole picture, then the assistants in his studio would paint the clothes the sitter was wearing, and the master himself would do the head and perhaps the hands and the finishing touches. Sir Anthony van Dyck (1599–1641), who had trained in Rubens' workshop and was one of the best-known and most successful British portrait painters in 17th-century England, had everything very well organized. With the sitter in front of him, he used to set down his ideas for a new portrait on a little piece of blue paper. Then the design was marked out on the canvas by assistants. The head would be painted by Van Dyck himself, and most of the costume by the assistants in his studio.

Sir Peter Lely (1618–1680), another very successful English portrait painter, went even further. He had a "stock book" of patterns for poses and clothes, from which the sitter could choose. Lely painted only the sitter's head, and then told his assistants to paint, for example, "whole length No. 8 and clothes No. 1." It was almost like painting by numbers—or ordering a meal in a Chinese restaurant! Another painter said, rather maliciously, that all Lely's pictures were "brothers and sisters," meaning that they all bore a family resemblance.

Sometimes in museums and art galleries you see a label saying: "from the Workshop of X [famous name]," or "School of Y [another famous name]." This means we don't know who painted it, but we do know that X or Y had something to do with it. He or she may have painted parts of it; or the person or people who did paint it may have learned from X or Y.

Here you can see a number of objects, all having to do with animals. They are made out of many different materials—that is, they use different media. See if you can guess which material goes with which object.

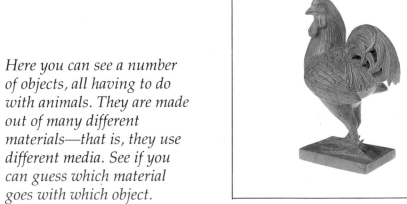

From Eggs to Concrete

It's easy to think of art as something only to do with paint and paper or canvas, with wood or stone, with clay or metal. But you can use anything you like to make art. Look back through this book and see how many materials have been mentioned. You might make a list of them. (You ought to be able to find at least 30.)

Here are some of the things artists use in different parts of the world. You can probably think of more to add to the list.

eggs	wool	ice	copper
rope	bark	gemstones	plastic
bronze	straw	reeds	brass
stone	gold	bone	sand
coconut	wax	concrete	glass
silk	ink	skin	chalk
clay	wood	paint	leaves
tea	charcoal	roots	nylon
snow	soapstone	iron	milk

If you use poster paints mixed with water to paint a picture on a piece of paper, you'll end up with a very different picture from the one you would produce if you used egg and water to mix colors ground from berries and metals to paint a picture on a wooden panel. (Before oil paints were invented in the 15th century, artists used "tempera"—the egg-and-water way of mixing paint.)

Artists have used the oddest things to paint or draw with, and to paint or draw on. There was a French artist who had the habit of drawing with a plug of tobacco he took out of his mouth. The English artist Augustus John dashed off a portrait of a friend on a tablecloth. And many artists have used junk—as Picasso did when he made a bull's head out of a bicycle seat and handlebars.

Before paper was invented, people used other things to draw or paint on. The ancient Egyptians used papyrus (made from a kind of grass), wood, or clay. In the Middle Ages and at the time of the Renaissance, painters used prepared wood (as Sassetta did in his painting on page 34). The medieval Books of Hours, like *Les Très Riches Heures du Duc de Berry* (page 63), were made of vellum (from calfskin). The Japanese and Chinese paint on silk. The Australian Aborigines often painted on bark, since there was plenty of it around.

(Right) David Kemp was asked to make a piece of sculpture for a special exhibition for children in London in 1990—and this is what he made. He saw the possibilities in two old boats, just as Picasso saw the possibilities in parts of an old bicycle.

Our hands are the most basic tools we have for art. A little boy in Peru made the picture below with just his hands and paint. He chose the colors very well.

(Left) Michelangelo, who lived in Italy about 500 years ago, liked to use marble for his sculpture. Many of his sculptures showed exactly how he worked on the marble, how he cut out the rough shape, how he used a big chisel for the background and a fine chisel for bodies, and how he polished some parts, like the faces, very smooth.

86

Drawing

Artists use drawing—with charcoal, chalk, pencil, or pen—for three main purposes. The first is as part of their training. The second is for keeping a sketchbook, like a private diary, of everything they think they might want to use. And the third is to create a picture—for other people to look at.

Learning to Look—Through Drawing

Like Dürer in the 16th century and Henry Moore in the 20th century, artists have spent a good deal of their time making drawings. Dürer used to dig up a chunk of dirt and grass, bring it into his workshop, and then draw it from many different angles. Moore made countless drawings of an elephant's skull, or of sheep in the different seasons, of Stonehenge, of pebbles . . .

In the European art schools of the 19th century, drawing was the most important subject. Students started off by drawing copies of engravings (which were already copies of other pictures). Then they moved on to making drawings of plaster copies of Greek and Roman statues. A student was not allowed to pick up a brush to paint, or to make a model for sculpture, until he or she had thoroughly mastered drawing.

Paper: A Great Chinese Invention

Paper was invented almost 2,000 years ago by the Chinese. It was made of the bark of the paper mulberry tree. But it was not made in Europe until about a thousand years ago—by the Arabs in Spain. They had learned the technique of paper-making from Chinese prisoners of war. Europeans had been rather slow to learn—the Maoris in the Pacific and the Aztecs in Central America knew how to make paper before the Europeans. The oldest piece of paper made in Europe that we know about is a letter from King Henry III of England dated 1216.

Paper gives artists the chance to do many different kinds of work. Some paper from China (made by hand from rags) has such a definite and varied texture that the paper itself can become part of the picture.

Some 20th-century artists—Klee and Picasso, for example—sometimes used newspaper to paint on, or included pieces in their pictures. Juan Gris (1887–1927) did the same with wallpaper.

In the 1960s, most art schools stopped teaching drawing. Later, people began to realize that students were not being taught how to *look*—which is what drawing does for you. Then artists like David Hockney (born in 1937) started to say what a good thing copying was, because you had to look through somebody else's eyes. People started to listen—to him and to others. These days drawing is back in the art schools.

Never Without a Sketchbook

Artists, like writers, often need to jot down ideas, record things they've noticed, note down ways of solving problems they're working on. Artists' sketchbooks are fascinating to look at—partly because of the way all sorts of unlikely things jostle together. We feel we're being let in on the ways artists go about their work, and allowed to see their private reactions to things.

Leonardo da Vinci was brimming over with ideas on all sorts of subjects, and filled many albums with drawings and notes. There are observations of the natural world—drawings of how water flows, studies of the structure of a bird's wing, plans for a flying machine (over 400 years before the Wright brothers!), drawings of hair, of a child in the womb, of details of buildings, and so on.

Dürer kept a day-to-day picture diary of people and places when he made a journey from Nuremberg to the court of Charles V in the Netherlands, to ask for his pension to be renewed. (He got the pension, and we still have his diary.)

Perhaps the biggest collection of an artist's sketchbooks that we have are those made by the English landscape artist J. M. W. Turner (1775–1851). Turner was fascinated by light and its effect on color. His sketchbooks are full of tiny watercolors, lovely in themselves, with thumbnail drawings of clouds, and notes to remind him of the colors. He once had himself lashed to the mast of a ship in a storm so that he could see the effect of the light on the water. (He must have had a waterproof sketchbook that day!)

Drawings for Others to See

Many artists have enjoyed drawing so much and found it such a good medium, especially for showing people's characters, that they have looked on their drawings as complete pictures rather than as preparation for something else. Look at the drawing on the right, and those by Rubens (of his son) and by Dürer (of his mother) on page 48, and you'll see why.

On one of his sketchbook pages, Leonardo da Vinci drew the face of St. James, one of the figures that he put in his famous painting The Last Supper. *In the corner of the same page is part of a castle.*

Drawing of a girl by Gwen Raverat (1885–1957).

Fast Frescoes

Artists not only make small drawings and sketches to prepare for easel paintings and for sculpture, but they also make full-scale drawings on a wall for mural paintings. These are paintings done directly on a wall (*murus* is Latin for "wall"). In Crete 3,500 years ago, tombs and palaces were decorated with murals. The Romans used to decorate the rooms of their grand villas with murals about 2,000 years ago.

In Italy in the 14th and 15th centuries, artists also painted murals—in churches, chapels, and government buildings—but using a special technique. These paintings were called frescoes (*fresco* is Italian for "fresh, wet,"), because the paint had to be put on while the plaster was still wet. Painting a fresco must have been very exciting work. There might be two, three, or four walls to be painted. So artists had the chance to make a very big and bold design. They had to work fast and not make mistakes.

(Above) *This 15th-century book illustration shows a girl sketching the design of a fresco on a wall. Women did paint in workshops but their names did not appear on the paintings.*

(Right) *This woodcut (from about 1500) shows a fresco painter in a rather dramatic situation. The devil is pulling him off the scaffolding, but he is saved by the Virgin Mary. She steps out of the fresco to catch* him by the hand. People at that time believed in the power of religious pictures. Notice the painter's equipment beside him which includes a T-square, paint, pots, and brushes.

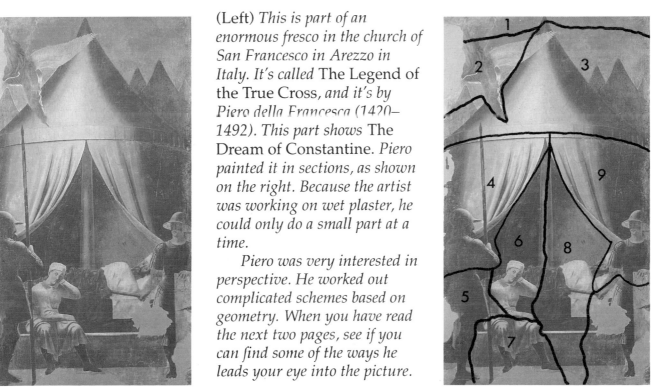

(Left) *This is part of an enormous fresco in the church of San Francesco in Arezzo in Italy. It's called* The Legend of the True Cross, *and it's by Piero della Francesca (1420–1492). This part shows* The Dream of Constantine. *Piero painted it in sections, as shown on the right. Because the artist was working on wet plaster, he could only do a small part at a time.*

Piero was very interested in perspective. He worked out complicated schemes based on geometry. When you have read the next two pages, see if you can find some of the ways he leads your eye into the picture.

Perspective—A Way of Showing the Real World

Perspective is one way of looking at the three-dimensional world and showing it in two dimensions. But it's not the only way of doing this. It's been particularly important for artists in the Western world for the last 600 years or so. But artists did without perspective for thousands of years, and many choose to do so now.

You've come across several examples of artists using perspective in the pictures in this book—though you may not have realized it. There are a couple of important points to understand about perspective.

1. The farther away things are from you, the smaller they look.

Look again at the photograph of the girl on page 5. The reason you knew that the little man was not dancing on her finger, but was on the far side of the field, was because he looked so small. You already knew from your experience of looking at pictures that things in the distance look smaller than things close up. (This is true even though the thing in the distance may really be bigger than the thing close up.) When artists want to show a scene in a "real" way—to make it look the way we see it—they also do this.

Look at the painting by Mary Cassatt on page 65, and then at the sketch of it this page. The biggest thing in the picture is the boatman—because he's nearest to us. The next biggest is the woman with the child on her lap—they're farther away, at the far end of the boat. Way in the distance, on the far shore, we see some houses. They look tiny—smaller than the boatman's ear. We know that houses are really bigger than ears. But because we know things in the distance look smaller, we have no difficulty in understanding that the houses must be a long way off.

2. Lines lead the eye into the distance.

Look at the diagrams above right. Imagine that they're floorboards. Look at Diagram A. You're standing in the middle of the room, and the floorboards are coming together and disappearing into the distance to a point on a line we call the horizon. That point is level with your eyes. In Diagrams B and C, you're standing first on the left and then on the right. In each diagram the floorboards go to a different point in the distance (but still level with your eyes).

Now look at the *Sunday Afternoon* paintings on pages 16–17, and the sketch of it on the next page. Look for the lines

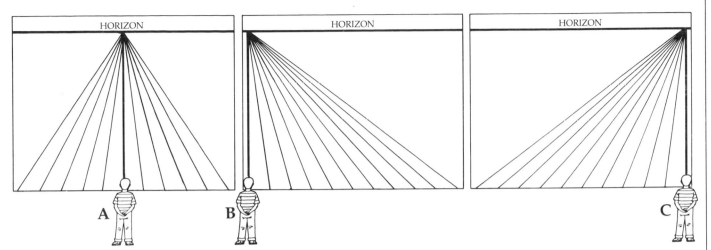

A B C

of the riverbank, the people, and the trees. You'll find that your eye is led to a certain point in the distance, on the horizon. This gives you an idea of how artists can compose their pictures to make you see things and

people at different distances, even though the surface of the picture is flat. It's in two dimensions. But the scene that the picture shows appears in three dimensions—it has depth.

At the time of the

Renaissance, artists worked out complicated perspective schemes based on geometry. Look at Piero's *The Dream of Constantine* on page 89, and see if you can figure out how he leads you into the picture.

Working in a Studio

Although artists were employed in painting whole walls or ceilings, many of their paintings were much smaller and were painted in a workshop or studio. In the past, successful artists often had many assistants to help them. But by the 19th century, it was usual for an artist to work alone in a studio. The studio might be only a cold little attic. Or it might be a specially built studio, with big windows to let in light from the north (the best light for painting), and with equipment such as easels, racks for storing canvases, and a platform for a model to pose on. Some 19th-century studios were quite luxurious. They were places where the successful artist would not only paint but would also entertain friends and patrons.

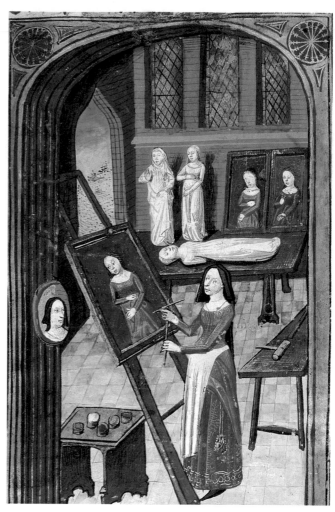

(Right) *A 15th-century woman artist is painting a picture on an easel. She seems to be looking at herself in a mirror, but the picture she's painting is not a self-portrait. She has her pots of pigment on the table by her side. The stick she's using to support her right hand is exactly the same kind that artists use today.*

In his workshop Dürer had a rather complicated drawing frame to help him with his perspective. It consisted of a movable eyepiece and a piece of glass in a frame on which the artist painted. The artist moved the eyepiece until he could see through the glass as much or as little of his subject as he wanted to draw or paint. He then traced the outline onto the glass. If he wanted to paint a picture from this, he could transfer it onto a canvas.

This oil painting by Monet, The Beach at Trouville, *really was painted on the beach. Monet was spending a vacation in Trouville with his wife, Camille (on the left), and their small son, Jean. Perhaps the little red beach shoe on the chair belongs to Jean.*

This photograph (much magnified) of a detail of the painting shows sand from the beach stuck in the paint, blown there by the wind that is flapping the flag in the background.

Working in the Open Air

Ever since the 18th century, when artists took to painting pictures of landscapes, they had made sketches on the spot, outdoors. But it didn't occur to them to paint the final picture itself outdoors. "Real" painting was something you did in your studio, with all your paints and equipment at hand.

But when the Impressionist painters began to experiment with color and ways to show light, they found they wanted to work outdoors. It wasn't just a question of the light. They felt that somehow work done outdoors was more "honest" and "true." They could observe nature closely, and catch the quickly changing effects of the weather.

It became the fashion to work that way, and to use lightweight equipment that could be folded up and easily carried around. The new paints, based on chemicals instead of natural pigments, were in tubes, and convenient to pack. But many of the Impressionists took their paintings back to their studios to finish them. Claude Monet (1840–1926) said he never had a regular studio. He used a boat. Later, when he lived in the French countryside at Giverny, he had a room built that served as both studio and living room.

This painting by Edouard Manet (1832–1883) shows Monet in his boat, which was set up as an outdoor studio.

Working with a Computer

Today people are experimenting with computers in making pictures. Using a "painting" software program, you can "paint" a picture directly on the screen, trying colors out, moving shapes around, enlarging and reducing them. Then you can print the picture you have produced, or you can use this plan as the basis for a picture, which you can draw or paint in the usual way. You can also make the computer produce repeated shapes and patterns which build up into a picture. This is called computer-generated art. And of course it can be sent (electronically) to other computer users.

Architects, engineers, and designers of books and TV graphics also find a computer a wonderful tool in their work. The great advantage is that shapes and lines can be moved around with great speed and precision many times over.

If you haven't yet tried out one of the computer painting or graphics programs, it's worth finding someone who will let you use one. The speed and freedom to experiment are exciting. As a tool in art, the computer seems a very long way from Dürer's drawing frame.

This is a picture made by the British artist Deirdre Borlase using a computer program. First she printed it right off the computer. Then she tried photographing it from the computer screen and copying the photograph on a color photocopier. The second way, shown above, gave a better result.

Today many artists have started to use computers—both to help them plan the composition of a picture, and also actually to "paint" the picture. Here is part of a computer graphics program. The signs on the left are the "icons" that tell you what computer "tools" you can use.

9 • Artists Earning Their Living

Poor as a church mouse? Rich as a business tycoon? Artists have been both—and still are. Mostly they have been somewhere in between. But in many parts of the world, artists have not been thought of as people who "earned their living" at all. No one in the community thought of paying the shaman who made a mask for a Native American ritual dance, or the African carver who made a wooden head, or the Australian Aborigine who made a bark painting. They were thought of as special members of their group, since they made sacred art. They were either supported by the group, or did ordinary work, such as hunting, as well. Where art is sacred, artists are sacred. They weren't doing a job as artists, in our modern sense, at all.

This tiny picture (made in about 200 B.C.) of a Greek sculptor working on a head is carved on a gemstone.

Earning a Living the Hard Way

When we look at some of the Greek statues, carvings, and pots that still exist, we can't help thinking that the people who made them must have been honored and respected. But it wasn't always so. The rich Greeks who lived in Athens about 2,500 years ago, and talked endlessly about politics and philosophy, were snobs when it came to artists. The wealthy Athenians thought of artists as low-level workers, engaged in dusty and dirty jobs—chipping away at stone, sweating in metal foundries. They were just men working for their living.

Over the next century, things changed in Athens. Architects and sculptors came to be treated more as equals by those who employed them. They were no longer just workmen, but were respected artists. Many of their names have come down to us today. Phidias, who made the great statue of the goddess Pallas Athene for the Parthenon, the hilltop temple in Athens, was one of the best known, though not one of his own works exists today—we only know his work through descriptions and later copies made by the Romans.

This picture of an ancient Greek bronze foundry, with sketches on the wall, is from a Greek bowl (made in about 480 B.C.) shaped like the one below.

This 13th-century Benedictine monk is painting a statue of the Virgin and Child. He is holding in his left hand a dish of paint, and the rest of his tools are on the floor. The picture (measuring 10 by 8 inches, dated about 1260) is painted on vellum and comes from a religious book made for Lady Eleanor de Quincy. Now it is in the library of the Archbishop of Canterbury, in London.

Working for Religion

Much of the art of the Middle Ages was made by monks working in monasteries. Some monks were given the tasks of farming, looking after the fishponds, or making honey. Others were given the work of copying manuscripts and illustrating them with illuminations. We don't know the names of most of these artist monks, but it's possible to recognize the style of one illuminator or another when comparing a number of manuscripts. The Books of Hours and other religious books that they worked on were sometimes specially commissioned as engagement or wedding presents. Not all the makers of religious books were monks; some were "lay scribes"—that is, ordinary people working in the monastery.

Women Artists

Although more attention is given to men artists of the past, there *were* women artists too. We even know some of their names. For example, there was Mabel of Bury St. Edmunds, in eastern England, a well-known embroiderer who worked at the king's court between 1239 and 1244. We have records of two women in London in the 14th century, a gilder called Dyonisia La Longe and a weaver called Matilda Weston, who combined their crafts with running alehouses! (A gilder is someone who puts gold on objects.) There was another Matilda, the widow of John Myms, who in her will left all her materials for making pictures to her apprentice, William. The fact that she had an apprentice tells us that she must have been quite a successful painter. But on the whole, women at that time worked not as artists in their own right but as members of a family business. They either did the hard work as assistants, such as carrying heavy materials or doing the plastering, or, if they were of a higher class, helped manage the business affairs of their husbands.

Here is a miniature of a woman also painting a statue of the Virgin and Child, about 500 years ago in France. Look carefully at the bench on which she has laid her tools and paints. Those small things nearest to you that look like seashells are just that—oyster shells. Painters used them as cheap palettes to hold their paint.

Working for a Patron

During the Middle Ages in Europe, the Christian Church was the greatest patron of the arts. Work might also be commissioned by a king or queen, a noble lord or lady, but this too was mostly for a religious purpose.

By the 15th century (at the time of the Renaissance), with the spread of wealth to people in business and trade, a wider range of people commissioned works of art. Many wealthy rulers liked to have artists attached to their court to design whatever needed designing—palaces, chapels, frescoes, fountains, jewelry, or special furniture such as wedding chests. Rich bankers and merchants also commissioned artists to produce small stone and terracotta sculptures, to design marble floors, to paint religious pictures, and to create gold and silver objects for their homes. People liked to show off their wealth. So there was an enormous demand for works of art of all kinds. There was no "mass production," as we know it, at that time—things were made individually.

There were large numbers of painters, sculptors, and goldsmiths to meet the demand. At the beginning of the 15th century there were, for example, about 100 painters earning their living in Siena, a small city of about 25,000 inhabitants in Tuscany, Italy. That's one painter to about every 250 people.

Artists as Craftspeople

Being an artist in the 14th and 15th centuries—like being a carpenter or a tailor or a butcher—often ran in families. It was common for artists to marry into other artists' families, and in this way family businesses were built up. The Bellini family of artists, in Venice, is an example of this. Jacopo Bellini (1400–1470) left his sketchbooks in his will to his son Gentile (about 1429–1507), also a painter. When Gentile died, he left them to his brother, Giovanni (about 1430–1516), who became the most famous painter of the Bellini family. Those sketchbooks were part of the property of their art business. Father and sons even had a kind of family trademark that they put on their work.

Art was very much a business. Artists were not expressing themselves or their feelings about the world in the way that we think of artists doing today. They were craftspeople with particular skills, and they were in it as a trade, to earn a living. They were not even called artists, but painters, or sculptors, and so on, according to what they specialized in.

(Right) *This cutaway painting of a building (a miniature from northern Italy made in about 1450) shows different craftsmen at work. See if you can find the goldsmith, the sculptor, and the painter.*

Guilds

When a young artist had gained a good deal of experience, he hoped to be accepted by a guild. The guilds were in some ways like modern-day trade unions. An artist could not get important commissions unless he belonged to a guild. Sculptors often belonged to the same guild as stonemasons and carpenters. Painters sometimes belonged to the pharmacists' guild, because they bought their colors from pharmacists. The powerful and rich guilds often acted as patrons themselves, commissioning many works of art.

Prints and Reproductions

With our printed books and magazines, our TV programs and movies, our photocopies and faxes, it's very easy today to send images and messages not only from one person to another but also from one country to another. But 500 years ago, the only way to send a message was to send it by a messenger. The only pictures you saw were those immediately around you in your local church, castle, town hall, or wealthy neighbor's house. If you wanted to see work by a particular artist who lived somewhere else, you had to travel there. There were no art galleries, no handy postcard reproductions. At most, artists, or their assistants, sometimes made a copy of a painting to be sent to another patron, or to keep for themselves.

But in the 15th century, a "new" technique (invented 600 years earlier by the Chinese) started to become important in Europe. It was the woodcut, and it became part of the printing revolution. For the first time, it was possible to make several copies of one picture in black and white. It could be "re-produced,"—that is, made more than once. So more people could see it. The development of the woodcut, metal engraving, and other forms of prints enabled copies of artists' work to be sent from country to country.

Prints give artists another range of techniques for producing works of art. Prints also allow artists to sell more work. And they bring works of art to a much larger number of people.

There are two kinds of prints. The first kind is an image printed from a block or plate prepared by the artist; it's printed by the artist or by someone else under the artist's supervision. The second kind is what we call mechanical reproduction, which is done by a photographic method invented about 100 years ago. That is the kind of print you get on a postcard.

Making Prints

To make a woodcut or a wood engraving, you cut out a picture from a block of wood. Then you put ink on the raised surface of the image and print it by pressing paper onto the inky block of wood. (It's the same technique you use with a potato or with linoleum.) Woodcut (**1**) was made in 1568 by the Swiss artist Jost Amman, and shows an artist actually making a woodcut. The wood engraving called *Fool's Song* (**2**) is by Gwen Raverat. It is an illustration for a children's book.

An artist making a line engraving draws the design on a metal (usually copper) plate with a tool called a burin—a short steel rod with a sharp point. (The picture on page 103 is an example of a metal engraving.) Artists started to use this technique in Italy and in Germany at about the same time—in the middle of the 15th century. From this time until the 19th century, engraving was the main way of reproducing artists' work, and that was how their work became more widely known. It was also another way for artists to earn money.

100

1

2

3

4

The etching technique was invented in the 16th century. It can produce more varied effects. You take a metal plate and coat it with wax. You draw your picture on the wax with an etching needle. Then you put the plate in a bath of acid. Where the etching needle has scratched through the wax to the metal, the acid bites into the metal. Then you take the plate out, get rid of the wax, put ink on the plate and wipe it. Ink is left only in the grooves—etched lines—and will print on paper pressed tightly to the plate. The etching (3) is by Thomas Newbolt.

The word "lithograph" comes from the Greek word *lithos*, meaning stone. This technique was invented at the end of the 18th century. You draw on a special kind of stone or a metal plate with a greasy crayon. This drawing is then "fixed" with a chemical so that it won't come off, and the stone is wetted and oily ink rolled over it. The ink sticks to the greasy crayon parts, but not to the rest. Then using damp paper, you make a print from the stone (or plate). Honoré Daumier (1809–1879) produced most of his cartoons as lithographs such as the example above (4).

Artists at Court

Today kings, queens, presidents, and prime ministers are not very interested in commissioning works of art. Sometimes a government commissions a splendid new opera house, or a new art gallery or arts center—but these are all *buildings.* In the United States and many European countries, there is a program called "Percent for Art." This means that anyone putting up a new building must spend, say, 1 percent of the building's cost on works of art, inside or outside the building. This is one way not only for governments but also for businesses and industrial firms to act as patrons of art.

In the past, in Europe, such programs were not necessary. Not only kings and queens but princes, dukes, and popes had their own courts. Many were eager to commission artists, sometimes paying them to be "resident artists" at court.

Some artists traveled quite far to get commissions. Usually it was the most famous, "modern," and innovative ones who were invited to distant places. The Italian Leonardo da Vinci, for example, worked in the main art centers of his own country before moving to the court of the King of France. The Flemish painter Rubens moved between Germany and Antwerp in the Netherlands, worked in Italy for various patrons, and visited Spain and England (where he was knighted). Portrait painters—such as Holbein and Titian—were in demand in many different countries. But most artists worked close to home. Transportation and communication were very slow. This made it difficult for artists to hear about new things that were going on in art.

This amusing drawing, made in about 1565 by Pieter Bruegel the Elder, tells us a lot about what the artist (on the left) thought of the buyer of his picture. "You fool!" he seems to be muttering under his breath.

Battle with the Art "Pirates"

Artists in the 18th century benefitted a lot from the invention of engraving. William Hogarth (1697–1764) started out as an engraver; he made book illustrations and studied painting in his spare time. He married his painting teacher's daughter, and made a name for himself as a painter (look back at *The Shrimp Girl* on page 52). He made several series of paintings on such subjects as marriage, making fun of people's habits and criticizing social conditions. He then had engravings made from his paintings, and these were enormously popular. Many of them were reproduced illegally—without paying Hogarth any money—by "pirates." Hogarth had a great battle with the pirates, and eventually Parliament passed the Copyright Act, which protected artists' and writers' rights.

Exhibitions

William Hogarth also started an academy for teaching art, and this was the forerunner of the Royal Academy.

The Royal Academy of Arts in London was founded in 1768. It housed an art collection, ran an art school (which still exists today), and held a big art exhibition every year (a very popular and fashionable event, which still takes place every summer). This exhibition was a wonderful opportunity for artists to show their work. There were similar exhibitions in Paris.

Palaces of Art

The art collections assembled by the royal families of Europe were private. But the French Revolution in 1789 changed all that—at least in France. The works of art belonging to the royal family and to other aristocratic families were taken over by the new government. From now on these works of art were to be for "the people." Artists, too, began to paint not for the aristocrats and royalty but "for the people." So in 1793, the first real "people's art museum" came into being in Paris and would later be known as the Louvre.

A little later, the various states that made up Germany started to establish public museums that included paintings, drawings, and sculpture. The people who set these up thought of them as "palaces of art" or "temples of art."

This engraving (12½ by 19¼ inches) by P. A. Martini of the 1787 Royal Academy exhibition gives a good idea of how they used to hang paintings then, covering every square inch of wall. The president of the academy, Sir Joshua Reynolds, is showing the Prince Regent around. It looks like an enjoyable event—even for the children and dogs! (You can't take your dog into the Royal Academy these days.)

Opportunities for Artists

By the 1830s, museums were being set up that were geared toward providing practical help to artists. Across Europe, 14 cities had opened museums showing only modern art, and another 66 cities had included galleries of modern art in general museums. The "new rich" in Europe, the men who were successful in business and industry, were much more interested in buying works of art from living artists than in tracking down Old Masters to buy.

In the United States, after the Civil War, New York was said to be "bustling rich." A small group of New Yorkers decided that what the city needed was a museum that would show the complete range of the world's treasures. It was to be for "the popular instruction and recreation" of the people. Set up in 1870, the Metropolitan Museum immediately became enormously popular with the people of New York. By 1894, they had demanded a restaurant (rare in a museum in those days) and somewhere to park their bicycles!

Art Becomes Big Business

By the second half of the 19th century, it was the ambition of many successful businessmen to own a collection of paintings by living artists. By this time art dealers had established galleries of their own. These galleries became fashionable meeting places.

Richard Redgrave (1804–1888) was a popular artist in Victorian England. He liked painting pictures that told a story, like this one called The Governess. *What could have been in that letter to make her so sad? The girls skipping, in their pretty dresses, make a strong contrast to her dark figure. But the girl with the book has a more thoughtful expression—perhaps she realizes something is wrong.*

Of course, the success of the dealers depended on the artists whose work they showed. Victorian artists particularly liked painting scenes with a story behind them—the return of the soldier from a war, the couple leaving England on an emigrant ship, the faithful sheepdog at his master's deathbed. These were enormously popular and sold for large sums. Some were reproduced as prints and sold in the thousands. The happy result was that many of the artists who painted them earned a lot of money. No more cold attics for them, but grand houses and spacious studios.

The Great Collectors

It has been fortunate for the world that in the last hundred years some of the richest people, especially in the United States, have chosen to spend a good deal of their money—made in steel and oil and other industries—on art. The collections of men like Paul Mellon and Henry Clay Frick started off as private collections and ended up as public ones. These men simply gave them to the nation. Some also gave the houses in which the works hung. The collectors who bought modern art gave a great boost to the art market.

The collector who made the biggest mark on the art world in the second half of the 20th century was J. Paul Getty II. He created the Getty Museum in California, whose collection of painting and sculpture is being added to all the time, and established a foundation to help scholars of art history and education.

Many of the other great collectors in the 20th century have been Japanese. Some Japanese businesspeople are willing to pay very high prices for pictures—particularly those by the Impressionists. As of this writing, the highest price ever paid for a painting was $82.5 million in 1990, for *Portrait of Doctor Gachet* by Vincent van Gogh. Prices like this have made people ask what determines an artwork's value. The people who benefit from these high prices are usually not living artists. When van Gogh was alive, he found it very difficult to sell anything at all. It is the art dealers and collectors, and the art auction houses, that make money from the work of artists who are now dead.

What Makes Something Precious?

Pieter Wiersma was born in Holland, and remembers as a child of 3 or 4 always playing with mud. He used to come home with sopping wet feet, and his mother scolded him. When he grew up, he was still fascinated by sand and water, and started to build extraordinary castles out of sand. He builds them below the high-tide line. He knows that the sea will wash them away within 12 hours at the most. Sometimes he spends the night on the beach with the castle he has built. He photographs his castles before they disappear.

People used to think that what made a work of art precious was partly what it was made of. In ancient Greece, sculptors used the finest marble they could find for their statues, decorated them with gold, and used precious stones for their eyes. In Italy 500 years ago, large areas of religious paintings were covered in gold. The color used for the blue of the Virgin Mary's cloak, for example, was made out of a precious stone, lapis lazuli, ground down to a powder. In Russia, the cover of an icon (a religious picture of a saint such as the Virgin Mary) was made of gold or silver and often studded with gems.

People wanted their works of art to be made of precious materials, as many of them were for religious use—to put in temples, shrines, and churches. People thought that the more precious they were, the more they honored God. Although that idea is no longer so important, some people still find it difficult to swallow the idea that a pile of ordinary bricks, arranged in a certain way, for example, can be a real work of art or can mean anything.

Nobody in the Middle Ages would have thought a statue made out of old nails, however well done, was worth anything at all. A painting in a plain wooden frame, however good the painting was, would have looked cheap to most people even a hundred years ago. Of course, people did value a painting or a sculpture also for the artist's reputation, if he or she was well known and in demand. These days we think that it is only the skill of the artist, and his or her reputation, that make a work of art worth a lot.

Here Today, Gone Tomorow

In 1990, the artist David Hockney sent a big picture from the United States to a friend in England by a fax machine—in 48 sections! Lines on fax paper fade after a while, so Hockney made sure that his friend's machine could take special paper that did not fade.

Artists like Andy Goldsworthy (see next page) think of their creations as parts of nature—which disappear or wear away. Buddhists make beautiful and complicated patterns out of colored sand, and then sweep them away.

Art galleries and museums spend a lot of time and money on restoring paintings and other objects. Do you think they should?

How long do we expect art to last?

"A lily of a day
Is fairer far, in May,
Although it fall and die
*   that night,*
It was the plant and flower
*   of light."*

The English poet Ben Jonson (1572–1637) wrote that. Might this be true of art as well?

Andy Goldsworthy is an English artist who often makes sculpture not to last. He makes beautiful forms out of leaves and flowers, roots, stones, bones, sand, and mud. He has been to the North Pole and made fantastic sculptures out of snow and ice. After some time, all that's left of his creations are the photographic images of them. When you next have the chance, in the country or at the beach, try making your own sculpture from things you find around you—and take a photograph of it, as Goldsworthy does.

Here's an image of one that he's chosen for this book. He made it in Australia out of kangaroo and sheep bones.

Fakes

A work is only said to be a fake if the artist tries to pass it off as somebody else's work. Copies are not necessarily fakes. Artists who produce fakes do so for a number of reasons. The obvious reason is to make money. But another one is the sheer pleasure of fooling the experts. Some fakers are very skillful. They not only match the style of the artist they're copying, but they also make a painting look genuine by using paper, canvas, or wood of the right period, and treating the surface of the painting to make it look the right age.

Fakes are valuable when they are thought to be genuine works by some famous artist, but once everyone knows they're fakes, they're valuable in a different way—as fakes! There was even an exhibition in 1990 of fakes from the Renaissance to the present day.

What do *you* think about fakers? Do you think they are common criminals? Or do you think, if we're taken in, we get what we deserve?

10 • Why No Two Works of Art Are the Same

Why are no two works of art the same? In the world today there are about 5,400,000,000 people. Each of those people is different from everyone else. Everybody looks and behaves differently. And each person's brain has millions of nerve cells, arranged into billions of tiny electrical circuits. These circuits are different in different people—and they carry messages that can produce creative thoughts. If you think about that, you'll get some idea of the reasons for the enormous variety of works of art.

Learning from Others and Being Original

Even though people and what they create vary so enormously, artists are always learning from the work of other artists, and getting ideas from it. Today it seems very important for an artist to be "original," to produce work that's not like anyone else's, if he or she wants to become well known. In the past it wasn't always like that. As you've read in the last two chapters, artists from the time of the ancient Egyptians and Greeks until the 18th century in Europe learned their art and craft in the workshops and studios of other, more established artists. Also, artists were often given detailed instructions about what kind of artwork they were expected to produce for a patron or a customer. Only a very few artists experimented and struck out in new ways. They were the ones who moved art forward. Some of these we think of as geniuses. But now *everyone* is expected to be doing his or her own thing, to be original. At the same time, we know that anyone who produces art must be influenced by the art that has gone before—following it, or reacting against it.

A String of Horses

On the next few pages you can see examples of how people have seen and shown horses. The time between the oldest and the most recent example is about 2,000 years. They represent some of the purposes of art suggested in Chapter 2. When you look at these horses, think about which horse fits which purpose of art, remembering what you have learned in the rest of the book.

Why Horses?

Horses have an interesting shape and have a powerful effect on people. Linked with the stars (Pegasus, the winged horse, is a constellation of stars), and with gods and goddesses, they have also carried soldiers into battle, transported people, and added excitement to sports.

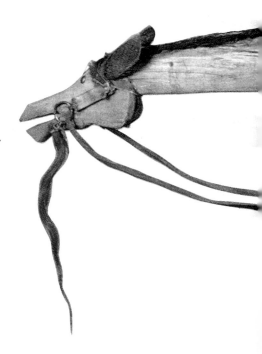

Superhorse

The white horse shown above is the biggest horse in this book. In fact, it's the biggest horse in Britain—365 feet from ear to tail. It's in Berkshire, in the south of England, and it's best seen from the air (as in the photograph). But the Celtic people who made it just over 2,000 years ago could never have seen it from the air, of course. So why did these people cut the shape of an enormous horse out of the green hillside, exposing the white, chalky earth? It's cleaned every 7 years, to keep it white, so it must have been "groomed" many times in its life! Can you think of any practical purpose the horse might have had? Could it have had something to do with the Celtic people's religious beliefs?

If you cut out the shape of a horse, you can't show any detail. You have to be able to recognize it as a horse from its shape alone. Try making a cutout horse yourself out of paper or cardboard, and you'll understand.

Sioux Horse

The galloping horse below was made by the Native American Sioux people out of wood, leather, and real horsehair. There can never have been a horse so long and thin, and yet we recognize it immediately as a horse. It gives us a feeling of speed. Perhaps this horse is more speed than horse—in the same way as some faces in Chapter 5 were described as "more feeling than face." Historians think this is a wounded horse. When the Sioux people celebrated a victory, they danced, praising the warriors and the horses that had been wounded in the fight. This carving may have been used in a victory dance. Do you think about it differently now that you know how it was used?

The Battle of the Rocking Horses

Take a look at the painting below. The horses in *The Battle of San Romano* by Paolo Uccello (who lived about 1396–1475), with their bright colors and perfect grooming, look more like rocking horses than battle horses. Uccello was one of the first painters in Italy to become interested in perspective. He was fascinated by its possibilities.

The picture is really an excuse for working out all sorts of complicated ways of showing perspective. Look at the dead soldier lying on the ground on the left, the lances of the soldiers on horseback, the path winding up the hills into the distance, and the small figures on it. Look back at the section on perspective on pages 90–91, and see if you can figure out how Uccello tells us about depth and distance in this picture. He has managed to make the horses stand out in a three-dimensional way, like carved and painted animals on a carousel.

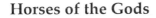

Horses of the Gods

In South India, outside Hindu village temples, you often find large figures of horses. These "belong" to the gods who protect the village. The horses can be life-size or even bigger, modeled in terracotta, and often painted. The two horses above are beautifully decorated, with plumes on their heads, neck ornaments, decorated cloths on their backs, and special saddles. They look something like circus horses.

111

Mystery Horse and Rider

This horse and rider are one. You don't get the feeling that the artist drew the horse first and then put the rider on it. He saw the two together as one shape. This horse is underfed and bony, his tail cut short. He and his rider make a mysterious and attractive pair. Somehow we know they're on a journey, not just out for a ride. Perhaps it's something to do with the wild landscape in the background. Imagine you're being photographed by one of those special cameras that make a map of your eye movements (see Chapter 1). How do your eyes move when you look at the picture for a few seconds? Is there one spot, or more than one, that your

eyes keep coming back to? Can you tell why?

For years people believed this painting, *The Polish Rider*, was by Rembrandt. Now some people think the painting is not by him, but by one of his pupils.

Wild Horse Head

The English artist Elisabeth Frink (1930–1993) had a country childhood with plenty of animals around her. Although she made sculptures of human figures and heads, she often returned to animals as a subject—particularly birds, dogs, and horses. She lived for 6 years in the south of France, where she saw the wild horses down by the sea in the Camargue. Her horses are vivid and horse-like, but not completely realistic. She once said of her work, "I use anatomy to suit myself."

She made this horse's head in bronze (24¾ by 31½ inches).

Horse Seeks Rider

On the right is a horse with a human use—look at its saddle and harness. It's standing ready to set off with its rider. This terracotta horse was made in China, probably about 1,300 years ago. It is 16¼ inches tall. Many horses like this one have been found, some of them glazed in green and yellow. They are called T'ang horses. The Chinese figure in Chapter 3 will give you a clue to the use of this horse.

Horse in Agony

This horse on the left is part of Picasso's painting *Guernica* (page 38) about the bombing of a town in the Spanish Civil War. There are many images of horror and suffering in that painting, including this horse. It's the kind of horse you might see in a nightmare. It's even like a horse you might see in a comic book.

In Chapter 5 you were asked to find out, by experiment, how the features of the human face express emotions. Try doing the same thing with a horse.

T the Black Horfe *in* Lumbard Street *Keeper of Running Cashes,* Humph. Stocks.

At the Sign of the Black Horse

Many businesses and stores have a sign that they hang outside and put on their stationery and advertising material. One of the oldest banks in Britain, Lloyds, has a black horse as its sign. The black horse sign goes back 300 years, to a goldsmith's sign in London. Compare the original shop sign (left) and the present-day symbol of the bank (above), and see what differences there are. In what ways do you think a horse used in a business sign should be different from a horse in an artist's painting?

11 • *Learning the Language of Art*

You probably know what this sign stands for. It is the sign of an organization that has to do with healing and caring: the Red Cross. The cross stands for the Christian religion. It is a sign that carries a message. In war, it could mean, *Don't fire on us! We've come to help the wounded.* This kind of sign-with-a-message is called a symbol. Symbols are like a special language or code that you learn to read.

In art, things often are not just themselves but stand for something else as well. The red cross is simple to understand because it is so well known, but symbols in art can be complicated. Understanding the symbols can make a picture more interesting and richer for you—can make you feel an emotion or teach you a lesson. But what if you don't know the language of these symbols? What do you do?

Learning something about the language of symbols is like going to another country and learning some of the language they speak there—you understand more about the people and get more from your visit. If you know something about the language of symbols, you'll understand better the people who made and looked at the pictures, and you'll enjoy them all the more. You'll probably find that you already understand some of the language of symbols without knowing it.

1

2

3

4

5

Find the Symbol

Symbols start with signs. It's convenient to have a sign for a business, for example, that people can recognize. In the past, masons had signs which they put on their stonework. Potters, sculptors, and painters often mark their work with signs. Many artists make interesting shapes with their initials—the example on the left is of Albrecht Dürer's monogram (**1**). Publishers are often recognized by their logos—like these from Viking (**2**) and Oxford University Press (**3**). Makers of pottery and ceramics usually have a sign they put underneath their wares. These are the signs of the St. Ives pottery in England (**4**) and the world-famous Spode pottery (**5**).

But a symbol is something more than a sign. A symbol can carry a message that is not just practical (as a logo on a book is). It can touch something deep in us. There are many examples of symbols in this book. You may not have noticed all of them, or may not have realized they were symbols.

Look, for example, at the stone carving from a French cathedral on page 56. The three men in bed are wearing crowns. Crowns are symbols of royalty—so you know the men are kings. The pointing figure has wings and a halo—so you know it's an angel. There's a star above them—so you know it's night. Because the carving is from a Christian building, we can guess the carving tells the story of the three wise men being warned in a dream by an angel.

Detail showing an angel, from a carving on a cathedral in France. (See page 56.)

In many Christian religious paintings you see different kinds of fruits and flowers, and often different kinds of birds as well. These aren't there just to make the painting look attractive, though they certainly do. Each is a symbol and has a special meaning. Many paintings of the Virgin and Child show Jesus holding a fruit, often an apple or a pomegranate. The apple is the fruit that Adam picked from the Tree of Knowledge in the Garden of Eden. It's a symbol for the Fall—the expulsion of Adam and Eve from the Garden of Eden, from Paradise. But the apple in the hand of Christ means that humanity will be saved.

Other symbols are more complicated. In his saltcellar on page 74, Cellini used the figure of Neptune (see detail bottom right), who holds the salt, to represent the salty sea, and a woman, who holds the pepper, to represent the earth (pepper is made from a shrub that grows in the earth). Neptune holds a trident (a three-pronged spear) in his hand. The trident is a symbol for the power of Neptune, the god of the sea.

Detail of Cellini's saltcellar, showing the figure of Neptune. (See page 74.)

But Beware!

The trident, as a symbol, has taken on many meanings. The trident has three prongs. The number three is very important in religion, so symbols that have three elements keep coming up. The ancient Greeks and Romans saw the trident as a symbol of lightning, the thunderbolt that comes from the thunderclouds to earth—a symbol of destruction. So the trident came to stand for Jupiter, the god who ruled the sky. For the Hindus it is the weapon of the god Shiva, the Destroyer. For Christians it can mean the Trinity (the number three again)—God the Father, God the Son, and God the Holy Ghost. It is thought that the fleur-de-lis, flower of the lily in heraldry, also comes from this shape. The fleur-de-lis is the royal sign of France, again a symbol of power. And you may have heard of the name given to a nuclear submarine—*Trident*. That certainly is a symbol of destruction and power.

So when you see a trident in a work of art, you need to know where that particular piece comes from and when it was made in order to fully understand its meaning.

Sun and Circle Symbols

Many symbols are based on our experience of the world around us. The most important is the sun, the source of light, warmth, and energy—the source of life itself. In many cultures it is associated with God's blessing.

The sun has been represented in many ways and with different meanings. The halo as used in Christian art is a symbol based on the sun, on light. It represents holiness and glory. When we look at Sassetta's painting on page 34, we know that the two old men must be saints because they have halos.

(Below center) *An Anasazi bowl from the American Southwest.*

(Below) *The design of the sundance lodge, used for ritual dances by the Sioux people in North America, is based on the circle.*

This ceramic plaque was made quite recently in Mexico. It is both a sun and a moon symbol.

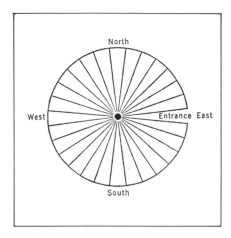

Halos

It's interesting to look at halos. They were painted in gold as flat disks until about 1450. In a crowd of angels, as in the painting on the right, they sometimes overlapped each other, or even partly blocked out an angel's face behind—as if the halos were solid. Quite often a halo had a name written on it (a great help in identifying the saint or angel, so long as you could read it). Christ, as in the mosaic on page 46, was often shown with a halo enclosing a cross. Sometimes a pope or an emperor, or even the donor of a painting, was given a square halo. Later, artists painted the halo still as a solid gold disk, but in three dimensions— worn rather like a hat, at an angle. Then they started to paint the halo as a simple ring of light. After the Renaissance, the halo turned into single rays of light radiating only from the heads of the Holy Family and God. And then artists stopped painting halos. Glory and holiness had to be shown in other ways.

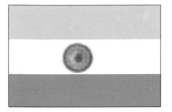

India

Japan

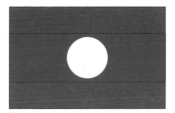

Laos

Uruguay

The sun is such a popular image that it shows up in all sorts of places. The pilgrim badge on page 70 shows St. Thomas à Becket in the center of a sun. The horse brass on the same page is another use of a sun symbol—to protect the horse from the evil eye. See how many other uses of the sun as a symbol for everyday things you can find. (*Hint:* look for the sunflower as well as the sun.)

The sun and the circle are closely linked as symbols. To the Native Americans of the American Southwest, for example, the circle has a sacred meaning. It represents the unity of life. They built large stone circles, "medicine wheels," for magical use. Circles and suns are carved on rocks, in the patterns on pottery and in baskets.

There are at least 14 countries in the world—including India and Japan, Uruguay and Laos—that have a sun in their national flag. (Stars are even more popular, with over 50 countries featuring a star or stars on their flag.)

The painting below (by a Neapolitanischer Meister, which means "an artist from Naples") shows the vision of St. John, as described in the Book of Revelation in the Bible.

Bird Symbols

Birds have also been used as symbols in many religions and cultures. For the ancient Egyptians, and other ancient peoples, they symbolized the soul which, according to their beliefs, flies away from the body at death. A bird can mean the soul in Christian symbolism as well. Different birds have different meanings. The Christ child is often shown holding a bird, usually a European goldfinch, a variety that has a red face patch. There is a legend that a goldfinch flew across the path of Christ on his way to be crucified, drew a thorn from Christ's brow, and was splashed with his blood.

If you look on page 81, you'll find a peacock on a tile. It could just be a beautiful decoration. But since it was made in Syria, and we know that the Syrians in the 15th century used a peacock to represent royalty, perhaps it means that this tile came from the palace of a royal person. In neighboring Persia (now Iran), the royal throne was called the Peacock Throne. To the ancient Romans, the peacock was the bird of Juno, the queen of the gods. The Roman empresses took it as their symbol. The Chinese emperors gave a peacock feather as a reward for good service. For the Hindus the peacock was the bird ridden by Subrahmanya, the god of love and war. In the Christian religion, the peacock symbolizes immortality and Christ rising from the dead—the bird's flesh was thought never to decay. In our everyday language it is associated with pride—we might say someone is as proud as a peacock.

This metal weathervane, in the form of a rooster, used to be on the spire of a church in the south of Germany.

Death was often symbolized by a skeleton figure carrying a scythe for mowing people down, as in this 15th-century woodcut.

In this detail from Holbein's painting The Ambassadors *(see page 67), the musical instruments could represent "the arts"—or death.*

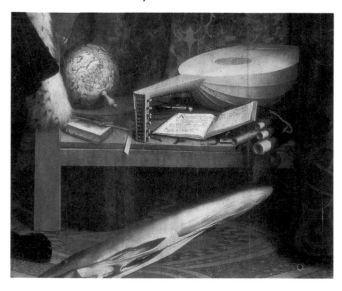

Everyday Symbols

Symbols don't appear only in religious paintings. In Dutch paintings of the 17th century showing scenes of domestic life, particularly those by Jan Vermeer (1632–1675), many quite ordinary, everyday objects have a special meaning. A jug balanced near the edge of a table is meant to remind us that life can end at any moment. Musical instruments may carry the message that earthly things must be left behind when we die. Of course, you don't have to understand the coded meaning in order to enjoy the painting. Vermeer's pictures are very easy to enjoy. But if you want to know what the people who lived during Vermeer's time saw in them, you need to know the code.

Signs and Their Stories

There is a spinning firework called the Catherine wheel. It was named after the Christian saint Catherine of Alexandria. She is said to have lived about 1,700 years ago. She angered the Roman emperor Maxentius because she wouldn't marry him and because she wouldn't give up Christianity. She debated with 50 philosophers—and she won the debate. So the emperor condemned her to be ground to pieces between four huge wheels. But before this could take place, the story goes, an angel destroyed the machine—and 4,000 people at the same time. Catherine became the patron saint of young girls and students, and of wheelwrights and spinners. The wheel is what we call her "attribute." You can recognize many figures in art by their attributes.

Another well-known combination of person and attribute which you see in many religious paintings is St. Jerome and his lion. The story goes that a lion came to the saint with a wounded paw. Jerome found a thorn stuck in the lion's paw and took it out. The lion recovered, became the saint's good friend, and never left him.

A medieval woodcut of St. Jerome and his lion (1483).

Speaking Through Gesture

Just as symbols have different meanings in different religions and cultures, gestures too can mean various things. They too can send messages. Artists can make the people in their pictures and sculptures "speak" through gestures.

In this book you can find several examples of hand gestures with different meanings. Look at the two hands poking out of the door in N. C. Wyeth's *McKeon's Graft (Train Robbery)* (page 14). Raised hands have become a kind of symbol for giving up, for making oneself defenseless, and for despair. The raised arms in Picasso's *Guernica* (pages 38–39) and Goya's *Third of May, 1808* (page 37) give the same message of despair and helplessness.

Even the small chess piece from the Isle of Lewis (page 82) shows a traditional gesture. The bishop is giving a blessing with his raised right hand. This gesture appears in many Christian works of art which show God the Father, Christ, or the saints.

Other cultures have a quite different range of symbolic hand gestures. The Hindu figure of Nataraja on page 61 shows the front right hand making a traditional gesture of reassurance. It means "Fear not."

This nativity scene from a 16th-century woodcut shows several "message" gestures: the king pointing to a star, the kneeling king folding his hands in prayer, and the Christ child making the gesture of blessing.

The Language of Color

Colors have their own symbolism. Gold represents something precious, and is often used by artists for pictures or sculptures of a ruler or a god. Halos were the mark of special beings, and represented holiness and glory; they too were often painted in gold.

There were other colors that were difficult and expensive to produce. Their message was the same: the object which they colored was precious. The Romans obtained purple by crushing the shells of rare shellfish. Purple was reserved for Roman emperors only. Medieval and Renaissance painters liked to use crushed lapis lazuli (an ornamental stone imported from the Orient) from which they made a brilliant blue. Artists used this expensive blue for the Madonna's cloak, to represent heaven. Artists wanted their paintings of her to be regarded as precious objects. The cloak that St. Francis threw away in order to become a monk is often painted blue, to symbolize the riches that he gave up for a life of poverty.

In medieval and Renaissance paintings of St. Francis and his followers, the Franciscan monks can be recognized by their brown habits and white belts with three knots, reminding the monks of their three vows of poverty, chastity, and obedience. The Dominicans, another preaching religious order, are often shown in paintings in their white tunics, which represent purity, and black cloaks, which represent their mourning for the death of the Virgin.

Colors have different meanings in different cultures. For example, in India white is the color of mourning. But in Western countries it is not white but black that is associated with mourning. In contrast, white stands for light, purity, and innocence. In Annunciation scenes, you may notice a white lily by the angel Gabriel—it stands for the purity of the Virgin. The white of the unicorn also represents innocence and goodness.

(Right) *This is another painting full of symbols. It is a watercolor by the 20th-century artist Paul Klee. He called it* Tree of Houses. *You can just enjoy it as a picture with lovely colors, interesting shapes, and a feeling of fun (like* Tomcat's Turf *on page 18). But you can also find in it some of the symbols mentioned in this chapter—and others as well. What could the houses mean? And the ladders? And why do you think there's a cross at the top of the tree?*

Time Line: A Pathway Through Art

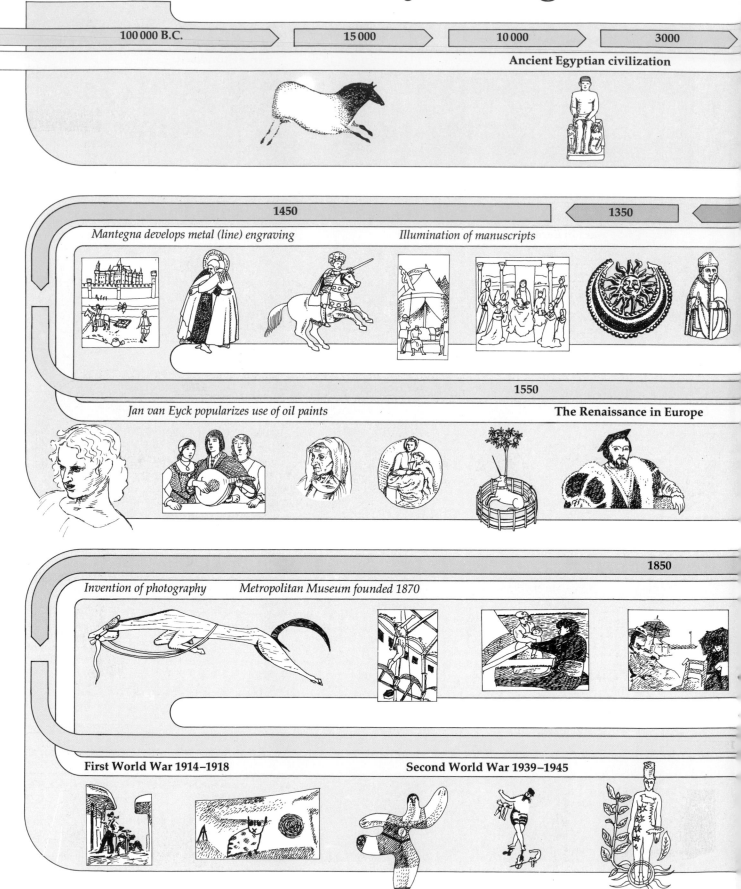

100 000 B.C.	15 000	10 000	3000

Ancient Egyptian civilization

1450		1350

Mantegna develops metal (line) engraving *Illumination of manuscripts*

1550

Jan van Eyck popularizes use of oil paints **The Renaissance in Europe**

1850

Invention of photography *Metropolitan Museum founded 1870*

First World War 1914–1918 **Second World War 1939–1945**

In this book you have read about many different kinds of art—some modern, some old. See if you can locate some examples here. Does this time line help give you a sense of the history of art?

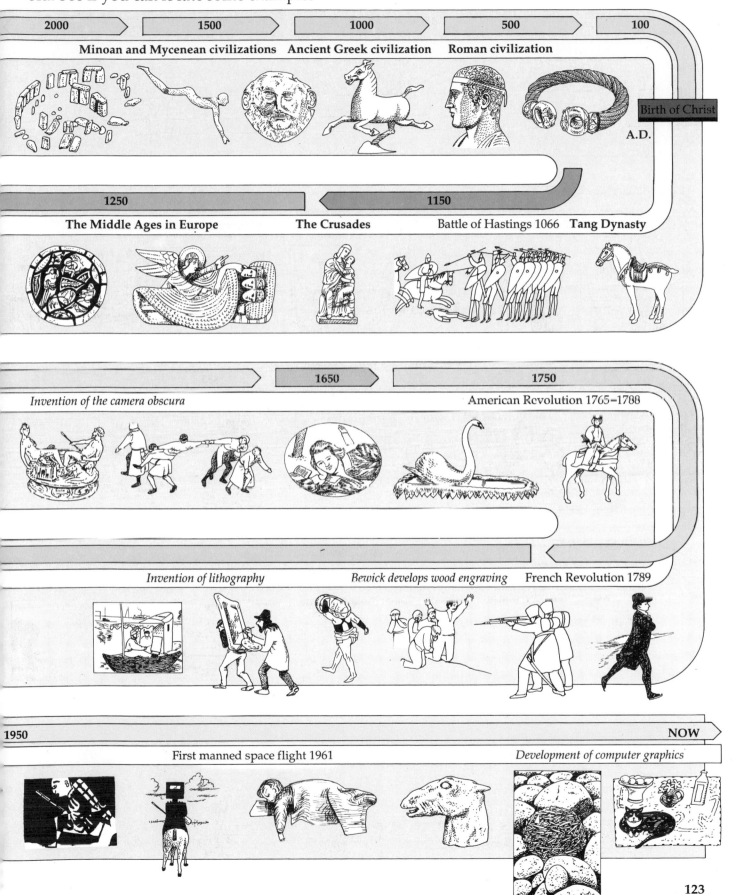

2000 · 1500 · 1000 · 500 · 100

Minoan and Mycenean civilizations · **Ancient Greek civilization** · **Roman civilization**

Birth of Christ
A.D.

1250 · 1150

The Middle Ages in Europe · **The Crusades** · Battle of Hastings 1066 · **Tang Dynasty**

1650 · 1750

Invention of the camera obscura · American Revolution 1765–1788

Invention of lithography · *Bewick develops wood engraving* · French Revolution 1789

1950 · NOW

First manned space flight 1961 · *Development of computer graphics*

123

Glossary

Acrylic ● A synthetic paint (that is, one not made from natural substances) invented in the late 1940s. Useful to artists because it dries more quickly than oil paint and can be used on nearly all surfaces.

Archeologist ● Someone who studies the past through old (often buried) buildings and cities, and the objects found in them, such as pottery, bones, coins, and jewelry.

Attribute ● An object associated with a particular person—often a saint in a work of art—and shown as his or her "sign." For example, St. Catherine's wheel.

Bronze ● An alloy (mixture) of copper and tin; used for casting figures originally modeled in clay.

Canvas ● Cloth, usually made of linen but sometimes of cotton, on which most oil paintings since the 16th century have been done. A canvas is stretched taut over a frame and prepared with a primer (first coat) before painting.

Cartoon ● Originally a plan or design for a picture. Nowadays, a single drawing, often an amusing caricature, of people or events, or a series of drawings (as in a comic strip) that tells a story.

Ceramics ● Objects made of clay or porcelain, usually painted and glazed. They range from the clay horses made by Chinese potters in the 8th century to be placed in tombs, to the most delicate porcelain bowls and cups made by European craftsmen.

Collage ● A picture or pattern made of pieces of paper, cloth, wood, metal, or any other material, shaped and colored to fit the artist's design, and stuck onto a canvas, card, paper, or wooden background. From the French word *coller*, "to stick."

Emblem ● An object (cross, crescent, shell, sun, etc.) or a figure chosen as a sign to represent an organization, company, occupation, or an individual or family—as in a coat of arms, or the shell of St. James.

Etching ● Method of making a print by drawing on a metal plate that is coated with wax, then dipped into acid and inked. Also the name for the print produced by this method.

Folk art ● The kind of art made traditionally by common people, often as decoration for things in everyday use. The same styles of decoration (flowers, leaves, birds, etc.) appear in many different parts of the world.

Fresco ● A wall painting made with pigment (color) mixed with water, which has to be completed while the plaster surface of the wall is still wet (or "fresh," *fresco* in Italian). Many were painted in Renaissance Italy.

Frieze ● A band, or strip, of decoration, made of plaster or painted wood, or carved in stone, in or on a building.

Gouache ● A watercolor paint to which white pigment has been added. Used by illuminators of medieval manuscripts and painters of miniatures, and popular today as an alternative to pure watercolor.

Hieroglyph ● In the ancient Egyptian written language, a figure or object representing what for us would be a word or part of a word.

Icon ● A painting or image of a saint or sacred figure of the Russian or Greek Orthodox churches. For believers, the icon itself is sacred. Also a small image used in a computer program.

Image ● In a general sense, all that you *see*. A drawing, painting, or model (in any material) of a person, or animal, or god or goddess, or an object.

Impressionists ● A group of artists (mainly French) who in the second half of the 19th century explored and tried to capture in paint their "impressions" of outdoor scenes in different light and weather. They often worked outdoors. They were particularly interested in light and color, and tried to use in their work scientific research on these subjects. The group included Manet, Monet, Renoir, Sisley, Pissarro, Cézanne, and Degas.

Line engraving ● Method of making a print by engraving an image on a metal plate and inking it. Also the name of the print produced by this method.

Lithograph ● Method of making

a print from a slab of stone, on which an image has been drawn with a greasy crayon. The stone is wetted and inked. The ink sticks only to the crayon lines. The print is called a lithograph.

Masters: the Great Masters or **the Old Masters** ● The phrase used for the most famous European artists (Leonardo da Vinci, Bruegel, Titian, etc.) of the period from the Middle Ages up to about the end of the l7th century.

Medium ● The material (paint, stone, clay, pencil, charcoal, etc.) chosen by the artist for a particular work. Also the liquid in which pigment (color) is mixed.

Middle Ages ● The period in Europe between about 1000 and about 1400. Also called the medieval period.

Miniature ● The name given to any tiny painting. In the Middle Ages it referred to illuminations painted on vellum in religious books.

Mosaic ● A picture or design made by cementing together small pieces of glass, ceramics, or stones of different colors. Often used for floors or pavements. Roman baths, palaces, and grand villas had mosaic floors, which can still be seen in some places where these buildings have been dug up—in the south of England, for example.

Mural ● A painting made directly on the wall of a building. A fresco is one kind of mural.

Oils ● Paint made of pigment (color) mixed with linseed oil or poppy-seed oil. First used in the 12th century, but not made popular until the 15th century by the Flemish painter Jan van Eyck. From the l6th to the 20th centuries, the most popular medium for artists. Oil paint can be put on in layers and used either thickly or thinly. It dries slowly, allowing the artist to make changes. It is good for painting details and giving an effect of three dimensions.

Palette ● From the French word for "little spade." A small portable tray, usually made of wood, on which an artist sets out colors and mixes them. It can also mean the choice of colors in the artist's work.

Perspective ● Method of showing on a flat surface (two dimensions) space and distance (a third dimension).

Pointillism ● A method of painting that uses hundreds of dots of different colors, which react together, when you look at them, more vividly than if the colors had been actually mixed together. It was invented toward the end of the 19th century by the French painter Georges Seurat.

Renaissance ● A period that began in the 14th century in Italy with a rebirth of interest in ancient Greek and Roman art and thought. (*Renaissance* is French for "rebirth.") The movement spread through Europe and inspired many great works of art.

Tapestry ● A woven wall hanging, usually made with a picture or pattern, particularly popular in the Middle Ages. Series of tapestries, which shared a theme or told a story, were often made to decorate a large room.

Tempera ● Paint in which the pigment (color) is mixed with egg. It was much used by Italian painters of the 14th and 15th centuries, particularly for painting on wooden panels. It dries quickly and gives less depth and variety of color than oils.

Terracotta ● Brownish-red clay that, when baked, can be used for pottery or sculpture. In some hot countries, terracotta bricks and tiles are used for building.

Totem ● A figure, often of an animal, adopted by different groups of Native Americans and others as the sign of their people, linking them to their ancestors.

Vellum ● A fine kind of parchment, made from the skins of calves, lambs, or kids; used for writing before the introduction of paper, particularly for illuminated manuscripts.

Watercolor ● Paint in which the pigment (color) is mixed with gum. When used, the paint is mixed with water. Since the 18th century it has been particularly popular with landscape artists.

Woodcut; wood engraving ● A print made by cutting out an image on a block of wood and inking it.

Suggestions for Further Reading

Cook, Janet. *Understanding Modern Art*. Tulsa: Usborne, 1992.

Cummings, Pat. *Talking with Artists*. New York: Bradbury Press, 1992.

Finn, David. *How to Visit a Museum*. New York: Harry N. Abrams, 1985.

First Impressions. Series. New York: Harry N. Abrams, 1990.

Gartenhaus, Alan. *Start Exploring Masterpieces of American Art*. Philadelphia: Running Press, 1992.

Greenberg, Jan, and Sandra Jordan. *The Painter's Eye: Learning to Look at Contemporary American Art*. New York: Delacorte, 1991.

Janson, H. W. *History of Art for Young People*, 4th ed. New York: Harry N. Abrams, 1992.

Keightley, Moy. *Investigating Art*. New York: Facts on File, 1976.

Looking at Paintings. Series. New York: Hyperion, 1992.

Papajani, Janet. *Museums*. Chicago: Children's Press, 1983.

Pekarik, Andrew. *Painting: Behind the Scenes*. New York: Hyperion, 1992.

Reener, Annee. *A Visit to the Art Gallery*. San Marcos, Calif.: Green Tiger Press, 1990.

Strickland, Carol. *The Annotated Mona Lisa*. Kansas City, Mo.: Andrews & McNeel, 1992.

Ventura, Piero. *Great Painters*. New York: Putnam, 1984.

Illustration Credits

Index